S0-ATC-437

Becoming

a

Historian

A

Survival Manual

for

Women

and

Men

1991 Edition by
Melanie S. Gustafson

Published by the Committee on Women Historians
and the American Historical Association

WITHDRAWN
EASTERN OREGON STATE COLLEGE
From EOU Library
LA GRANDE, OR 97850

1990 Committee on Women Historians

Joan Jensen, chair, Department of History, New Mexico State University; Barbara Melosh, Department of English, George Mason University; Robert Moeller, Department of History, University of California, Irvine; June E. Hahner, Department of History, State University of New York at Albany; Anna R. Clark, Department of History, University of North Carolina at Charlotte; Melanie S. Gustafson, Department of History, University of Vermont, Burlington; Noralee Frankel, Assistant Director on Women and Minorities, American Historical Association; Samuel R. Gammon, Executive Director, American Historical Association, *ex officio*.

Editor: Roxanne Myers Spencer
Pamphlet Series Editor: John Barnett
Editorial Assistants: Robert Townsend
                    Lydia Robinson

© 1991 by the American Historical Association

All rights reserved. No part of this book may be reproduced in any form without permission in writing from the publisher, except by a reviewer who wishes to quote brief passages in connection with a review written for inclusion in a magazine or newspaper.

ISBN: 0-87229-047-6
Library of Congress catalog card number: 90-0857-13
Printed in the United States of America

Copies of this publication are available from the American Historical Association, Publication Sales, 400 A Street SE, Washington, D.C. 20003-3889.

Contents

Author's Preface

Becoming a historian requires training, hard work, and the fulfillment of scholarly and professional obligations. Meeting these demands can be stressful. We hope this manual offers some alternatives to many of the stresses and tensions inherent in starting out in a new field. In addition to offering specific information to help you as you enter new phases in your career, we hope this manual will provide you with a benchmark for understanding other historians' professional positions and their aspirations and actions. Armed with that understanding, it is easier to downplay what appear at first to be somewhat threatening situations and to take pleasure in the highlights—and there are many—of your chosen profession.

Becoming a historian will be gratifying. Passing your comprehensive exams, receiving your first job offer, and having an article accepted for publication are some of the tangible rewards of the profession. Beyond those specific rewards are two somewhat less tangible, but nonetheless profound, rewards of becoming a historian: Professional autonomy and the satisfaction of performing services that few other professions offer are frequent and fulfilling rewards that accompany every phase of the dedicated historian's career.

We hope that *Becoming a Historian: A Survival Manual for Women and Men* emphasizes the privileges of living the life of a historian, as we hope it provides you with guidelines and incentives for professional satisfaction and success.

—Melanie S. Gustafson
Department of History
University of Vermont, Burlington
January 1991

Foreword

The history profession, like any other profession, operates in large measure by unwritten rules. Historians who have had no coaching in these folkways often have difficulty getting comfortable with their positions in the profession and in moving forward successfully as their careers progress. The American Historical Association's Committee on Women Historians (CWH), recognizing that unwritten rules often lead to inequity, has put together this manual to reveal the most important rules and customs of our profession. The first version of the *Manual for Women (And Other) Historians* appeared in 1975. This is the third revised edition, and the title change reflects its change in scope. This is a manual for all historians at the various stages of their careers.

The aim of this manual is to provide practical information that will help beginners become informed participants in the historical profession. The authors address men as well as women, but they comment on the particular circumstances faced by women because those circumstances sometimes require special attention.

The first version of this pamphlet was prepared by the 1975 Committee on Women Historians: Suzanne Lebsock, Mary Frances Berry, Carl Degler, Mary Jane Hamilton, Joan Kelly, Linda K. Kerber, Jane deHart Mathews, Emiliana P. Noether, and Marie Perinbam. They sought advice from a number of people, especially Otis Graham and Dorothy Ross. The second version was prepared by the 1979 CWH, Joan W. Scott, Judith Babbitts, Mary O. Furner, Rosalyn Terborg-Penn, Martha Tolpin, and Sydney V. James. A special debt is owed to Sydney James, who rewrote large sections of the text. The 1979 CWH: benefited from comments by Linda K. Kerber, Evan A. Thomas, Barry Karl, Janet W. James, Noralee Frankel, and Phyllis D. Keller.

This version of the pamphlet incorporates material from both previous editions and has been prepared by the 1989 CWH: Barbara Engel, Melanie S. Gustafson, Louise Kerr, Barbara Melosh, Robert Moeller, and chair Joan Jensen. Significant sections of this pamphlet were written and revised by individual historians, and we acknowledge their important contributions: Paul Boyer in Chapter 2, How to Apply to Graduate School, for "Tips on the

Personal Statement and Letter of Recommendation," which appeared in the October 1989 issue of the American Historical Association's newsletter *Perspectives;* Barbara Melosh in Chapter 6, The Job Search, for "Jobs with the Federal Government"; Linda Gordon in Chapter 7, Survival at Interviews, for "Successful Job Interviewing," which appeared in the November 1989 *Perspectives;* Barbara Engel in Chapter 10, Tenure and Promotion, for the section on promotion; Cynthia Harrison for information on jobs for public historians; Robert Moeller for Chapter 11, The Professional Couple; Joan Jensen in Chapter 14, Getting Published; and Linda Arnold, for "A Checklist of Job Interview Queries" in Appendix A. Much of the information in the Bibliography and in Appendix B, "Selected List of Professional Organizations," was taken from *Careers for Students of History,* by Barbara J. Howe, published by the American Historical Association and the National Council on Public History.

Noralee Frankel and Roxanne Myers Spencer of the American Historical Association provided insightful editing. We also thank Ellen Broidy, Mary Miner, and Cynthia Harrison for reading the entire manuscript and providing helpful comments.

1
What Makes History a Profession

The Purpose of this Manual

This is a manual about how to become a member of the historical profession and how to get along when you do. We hope to introduce you to the profession as a whole and to help you navigate the various phases of the profession, from the first decision to apply to graduate school through the tenure process. While not every section of the manual may be relevant to your immediate needs, we encourage all historians to read the whole manual at least once to get a sense of the needs of colleagues who are at different points in their careers. Then, focus more specifically on those parts of the manual that are of greatest concern to you now. We believe the entire manual will not only help you learn the folkways of the profession but also will help you to be a better colleague.

This manual should be relevant to everyone in the historical profession but includes material of special concern to women. Issues such as sexism, heterosexism, and racism also have been seriously addressed, and information of interest to gays, lesbians, and people of color has been added. Much of the manual is necessarily directed to academic historians, but an effort has been made in this edition to include items relevant to public historians.

The Professional Historian

Defining the profession

Let us begin with a stab at definitions. We use the word "profession" to refer to a certain kind of occupation and the aggregate of people who pursue it. Historians study and propagate knowledge about the human past. They must be aware of where their individual occupation fits into the collective existence of the profession. Whatever service they perform—whether it is teaching, research, exhibit preparation, site interpretation, administration of historical programs, media production, oral history, or archival management—is based on the labors of a multitude of other historians. These efforts have been cultivated by using the historian's special skills. Most historians, in turn, have taught beginners. They have accumulated the knowledge that is the historian's province, invented ways to interpret it, and engaged in the controversies over interpretation that keep the profession alive. Any one historian, therefore, draws on the work of the others and should be prepared to take part in the collective endeavor.

A profession implies an organization, usually quite an elaborate one. Collectively, the practitioners decide their responsibilities and work to maintain those standards. In universities, a group of professional people accept candidates, train them, and decide when they are ready to practice. Successful candidates join associations, ordinarily of regional or national dimensions, but often with international ties, such as the Organization of American Historians, the National Council on Public History, or the American Historical Association. Collectively, the practitioners evaluate one another's contributions to learning. Professional solidarity calls for evaluating other historians purely on the basis of their performance as historians. All historians are obliged to keep abreast of the publication of new discoveries, carry forward research, evaluate other historians' work, participate in professional organizations, and disseminate historical knowledge.

Code of ethics

Like other professions, the historical profession has its own ethics. For historians, whose work is interpreting the human past, the first canon requires accuracy in its fullest sense. It is the duty of the professional to understand how the canons of accuracy, honesty, thoroughness, freedom from bias, and other ethical considerations are evaluated and defined within the profession. Publications defining these ethics include the American Historical Association's "Statement on Standards of Professional Conduct," and the National Council on Public History's "Ethical Guidelines for the Historian," among others.

Representing the profession

Historians have an obligation to promote the profession both internally and externally. Such professional service entails a host of corollary duties. Some are professionwide, such as advancing knowledge and putting it before the public. Other duties are more specific to the particular positions in the profession. Teachers must teach, editors must edit, managers must manage, in ways that satisfy the legitimate expectations of those who count on benefits from these services. The moral obligation to serve creates a special relation between work and pay, a special relation between the profession and the public. Our duties continue, regardless of the hours, until we have done our best to achieve professionally satisfactory results.

A working historian becomes part not only of the profession but also the larger academy. While disciplinary boundaries seem to be unchanging at the university level, many individuals may find that they often cross these boundaries as they conduct research, engage in debates, and build their communities and support networks. Interdisciplinary connection is particularly common for historians who concentrate in women's history, ethnic history, and gay and lesbian history. As a result, multidisciplinary groups defined by thematic interests have developed within the academy. Many historians may find that these multi- or interdisciplinary groups provide them with an additional professional community that suits their academic and professional interests. Public historians often find opportunities for scholarly engagement in interdisciplinary seminars held within public agencies or set up independently by scholars in a community.

External promotion is advanced by popularizing the study of history and by seeking public support for higher education, research, and historic preservation. Write to your congressional representative or senator to support larger appropriations for colleges and universities and for cultural endowment. Such efforts may also be effective in getting more historians employed.

The long hours many historians put into their careers result not only from their obligation to the profession and their interest in the past, but also from their understanding that they are part of a larger community working to make the world a more humane place. Historians are not so narrowly focused that all they do is eat, sleep, and think history. All historians have other interests and responsibilities. Still, the career of the professional historian sounds demanding. It is. It sounds as though it requires uncommon self-discipline. It does. It also, however, offers priceless rewards: professional autonomy and satisfaction in performing services that few other professions can offer. This manual provides historians with outlines and gauges for success in the diverse roles that they will play as professionals throughout their careers.

2
How to Apply to Graduate School

Deciding to Apply

To be accepted as a graduate student in history, start planning your applications almost a year before you wish to enroll. Ordinarily, that means in the autumn of the senior year in college. Deadlines for applications vary from early December to February, sometimes later. Plan to take tests, such as the Graduate Record Examination (GRE), because most schools want to see test scores as early as possible. Try to take the GRE in October but definitely take it by December. You need not give up hope if you take tests later, but you should realize that the main part of the selection process will be over by the time your scores are available. Most graduate fellowships are awarded in March, in time for the general announcement of admissions in April.

Gathering Information and Applications

The American Historical Association's *Directory of History Departments and Organizations in the United States and Canada* is usually available in your undergraduate school's history department office. The *Directory* provides information on almost all graduate history departments in the United States. Inclusion in the *Directory* is by subscription, so a few institutions are not represented, but by and large, this is a very comprehensive resource. You can find other educational directories, such as *Barron's Profiles of American Colleges* and *Peterson's Guide to Graduate and Professional Schools,* at your college or public library. Look at graduate school catalogs as well. Catalogs list courses offered as well as admission, degree, tuition, and financial aid requirements. Most of the information will be up-to-date, though changes in tuition rates and course offerings are frequent. You should be able to find catalogs in your school or public library. If not, the schools you are interested in will send them, although some graduate programs will only send a catalog after receiving an application or a fee. Try to collect catalogs from schools the summer before you begin the application process so that you can think about your choice.

Ask your undergraduate professors for information and find out if they will put in a good word for you with acquaintances in graduate departments. To get the most useful responses about graduate programs from your professors, pose questions in ways that allow for straightforward answers. Ask your professors which schools they think offer the best programs for your interests and abilities. Do not hesitate to seek out professors' advice, even if you have not taken classes with them. If you know someone who studied at a school you are interested in, that advice may be particularly valuable. Your undergraduate catalog will often list where faculty members did their graduate work.

To apply, you must have the necessary forms. These are available by writing to the individual schools. Address your request to the director of graduate admissions or the department of history if you cannot find a specific name. You will receive in reply a packet of forms and information. Then your real work begins.

What to Look for in a Program, Department, and School

Remember that you will be spending at least two years and probably far longer in the graduate program and department. The average number of years to complete the PhD in history is eight! Therefore, you should learn as much as you can about specific aspects of the department, its programs, and the institution. The following points will help you with decision making at both the application and selection stages.

Explore special programs such as those in archival management or women's history. If you are attracted by a special program within a department, such as legal history or the history of technology, do your best to find out whether the program is securely established. If you expect to depend heavily on one or two faculty members, find out about their status. Professors often leave for sabbaticals, move to other campuses or colleges, or retire. If your decision is based on a particular faculty member, know whether there is a backup person to work with should that professor leave. This becomes particularly important as you begin to select among the schools that have accepted you.

Find out about the dissertation topics and placement of recent graduates by looking at placement records, if they are available, or by asking the graduate adviser. Look at a list of recent dissertations, which the department should have available. For an overall view of recent PhDs, see the AHA's annual *Doctoral Dissertations in History,* and *Dissertation Abstracts,* published monthly by University Microfilms International, Inc. *Dissertation Abstracts* includes abstracts of doctoral dissertations submitted to UMI by 550 participating institutions, and it is available in most university libraries. Consult back issues of the Organization of American Historians' *Journal of American History,* which lists dissertations in American history. Dissertations granted within a department will reflect both faculty interests and the facilities available.

Identify resources for graduate students. Does the library have extensive holdings? Are there computers available for students? These resources indicate the level of commitment within the department and school.

Research financial aid and awards. Read the catalogs and any departmental brochures you can find. It is likely that only some awards are channeled through the department. Do you need different forms to apply to different grant offices? Find out if a first-year financial aid commitment is for one-time only or if it means that the department is committed to funding every year of your course work. Is there funding for dissertation research? You should weigh the nature of the financial aid package with the quality of the school. If possible, don't just go to the institution that offers you the most money.

If you plan to supplement your stipend (should it be awarded) with student loans, you will have to file financial aid forms with the financial aid office at each school. Most often these forms should be filed as soon as possible after the first of January. The sooner you file these forms the better. Most schools require additional information, such as a copy of your most recent tax returns and other verification materials. Each school's policy is different and you should contact the proper personnel for further information and forms. Do not rely solely on what the history department tells you. Call the financial aid office directly. The forms used by schools include the Family Financial Statement (FFS) from the American College Testing Program (available from your financial aid office) and the Financial Aid Form (FAF) or the Graduate and Professional School Financial Aid Service (GAPSFAS). (The latter two are available from the College Scholarship Service, a division of the Educational Testing Service. The address is listed in Appendix B, page 97.) Know which forms are required by the schools you are applying to. You might want to send your financial aid applications by registered mail, so you have proof of receipt in case of a financial aid dispute. Do not wait to be accepted to file these forms or you might miss important deadlines.

Clarify differences in the requirements for MA, PhD, and other special programs. Which should you be applying for? Is the master's degree a terminal degree or the first step to the PhD? Is there flexibility in the program requirements? What are the language requirements? If there are language requirements, try to meet them before you begin the graduate program.

Departments also have political colorations and biases in favor or against particular trends in history. Consult a professor in your own department whom you trust to be candid, and be sure to raise these questions.

Once you have become familiar with a school's official publications, don't hesitate to write, call, or visit to get further information. If you plan to visit a school, go to the best school for your purposes, not simply one that is cheaper or closer to where you are living when you apply. This is not the time for basing your decisions on short-term goals. If you cannot visit, contact the faculty member whose field is nearest to your interests. You can find out individual faculty members' office hours from the department. You might also ask the graduate secretary for names of current students in those programs. Students may give you a more candid assessment of the program's strengths and weaknesses. Make as informed a decision as possible.

Attempt to build relationships with prospective faculty advisers. Write to faculty members with whom you would most likely work. This initial letter should explain the kind of research you would like to do and perhaps include a copy of your statement of purpose. Even if these faculty advisers are not on the admissions committee, they might be able to go to bat for promising applicants.

After you have visited a department, met with professors, talked with graduate students, and gotten a feel for the community, write to thank the people you met. Remember, no matter what school you attend, these individuals will be your professional colleagues, so start building good will now.

The Application Process

Application instructions will vary with each institution, so read each set with care. Your application may be scrutinized by all members of the department you send it to, but usually it will be examined by a committee. Graduate admissions committees look for students who show potential for solid scholarship and who have a lively interest in history. Unlike college recruiters, they are seldom scouting for leadership talents or well-rounded persons. To increase your chances of acceptance, make scholarship the focal point of your application.

Tips on the Personal Statement and Letters of Recommendation

Together with the academic transcript and (in some cases) GRE scores, the most important components of an application for graduate study in history are, for many history departments, the student's own statement of purpose and the supporting letters of recommendation. Here are some suggestions for avoiding common pitfalls in their preparation and for making them as strong and persuasive as possible.

In brief, the most effective statements of purpose are those that are specific, well-written, professional in tone, scrupulously accurate in spelling and grammar, and tailored to each institution. The statement should avoid sweeping philosophical generalizations, avowals of political or other ideology, or ruminations about the nature of historical knowledge and its essential role in bettering the human condition. No matter how earnestly intended or passionately felt, such lofty rhetoric all too easily descends to the level of cliché, especially when offered in a necessarily compressed form, suggesting an immature and jejune outlook rather than the intended profundity. The statement should also avoid mention of extracurricular activities and achievements, no matter how outstanding, unless they have a direct bearing on the professional field to which you are seeking entry.

While it is certainly appropriate to discuss how you became interested in history, and to include something about your long-range career goals, such matters should be kept brief and to the point. Remember that your application is one of many being read by busy faculty members who have numerous other time-consuming obligations. Keep your tendencies toward loquaciousness well in check, and observe word limits strictly.

The strongest statement is one that sums up your scholarly interests and immediate academic objectives in a clear and straightforward fashion. It should be quite precise about the time period, geographic region, or kind of history you want to study, and perhaps even the specific topic you wish ultimately to investigate. You should briefly indicate how your undergraduate reading, research, and course work have shaped your particular interests and prepared you to pursue them further. At the same time, bear in mind that the earlier phases of graduate education involve primarily general training rather than research on a specific topic. Therefore, your statement should convey an openness to the acquisition of a wide range of historical knowledge and research skills rather than an obsessive fixation on a single narrow topic. (An application from a college senior whose sole purpose in life is to study the Battle of Antietam or the fall of Malacca to the Portuguese in 1511 would probably raise warning signals for most graduate admissions committees because the student may appear too intellectually rigid and narrow.)

It is entirely appropriate, indeed desirable, to tailor your statement of purpose to the institution to which you are applying. Feel free, for example, to mention professors with whom you would like to work, or specific strengths—such as particular manuscript holdings or degree programs—that make the institution attractive to you. Such specificity should avoid elaborate praise or flattery, however; a fawning, excessively deferential tone is likely to be counterproductive.

The statement of purpose is also the place for you to address briefly any anomalies or ambiguities in your record that might give an admissions committee pause, such as a nonstandard grading system or courses whose content is not clear from the transcript (such as, "Independent Study"). If your undergraduate background in history is weak, it might be advisable for you to describe in more detail the evolution of your academic interests and to make plain that your commitment to the discipline is now firm.

The quality of the essay is probably more important than its substantive content. The members of the admissions committee who read your application will evaluate your statement for the evidence it offers about the quality, clarity, and originality of your mind; your maturity and sense of direction; your skills as a writer; and your capacity for careful attention to detail. A thoughtful, well-crafted, coherently organized essay can go a long way toward favorably disposing a committee on your behalf. Conversely, a shallow, formulaic, hastily written statement marred by poor organization, awkwardness of expression, or (even worse) outright grammatical errors or misspellings can seriously undermine an otherwise strong application. There have been instances of application essays where misspelled words or grammatical errors had been heavily circled or underlined by previous readers, with an exclamation point in the margin. Such lapses of detail are not necessarily fatal in themselves, particularly if the admissions committee convinces itself that the applicant is "a diamond in the rough." But such errors are sufficiently damaging, especially in borderline cases, that every effort to avoid such mistakes is strongly recommended.

Letters of recommendation are also highly important. You should select with great care the professors you ask to write on your behalf. While you obviously cannot quiz someone in detail about the content of a letter of recommendation, it is acceptable for you to ask in advance whether the professor feels able to write a reasonably positive letter. If possible, select faculty members whose scholarly work might be known to those who will be reading the letters. (Admissions committees evaluate the writers of recommendation letters as well as the subject of those letters!) Sometimes, particularly at large institutions, it is junior faculty members, or even graduate teaching assistants, who know the applicant best and who write the most useful and perceptive letters. Where feasible, however, try to supplement letters from beginning or relatively unknown instructors with others from more established scholars.

Generally speaking, try to secure a letter of recommendation as soon as possible after you have completed a course or independent study project, when you and your work are still fresh in the instructor's mind. If you wish to obtain a letter from a professor with whom you studied a year or so in the past, or who taught you in a large lecture course, spend a little time talking about your work in the course, your general undergraduate program, and your scholarly interests, to refresh the instructor's memory and fix yourself more precisely in the writer's mind. The more specific a letter of recommendation, the greater the weight it tends to carry.

Clearly, no single formula can guarantee admission to graduate school in history or any other discipline. Each admissions decision reflects a variety of factors and subjective judgments by fallible human beings. But the tips offered above should maximize your chances. Good luck!

Forms and Deadlines

If you feel it would be helpful, you can devise a simple form for requesting recommendations. Include such pertinent information as your grade point average, any scholastic honors achieved, brief statements of your purpose in requesting the recommendation, and a personal assessment of your goals and your ability to fulfill them. This form can be submitted to professors to help them prepare a recommendation. If such forms are already available at your institution, make sure that you fill in the necessary information, and sign it if required. Allow ample time for professors to send the letter before the deadlines, and always include a stamped, addressed envelope. Before the deadline, verify that the school received your letters. You might need to remind the professors of the deadlines.

Transcripts

You will be asked to send transcripts or to have your college send them as soon as possible. If your transcript does not follow a standard format, insure that it is accompanied by a description. If courses are listed in obscure abbreviations, send along a prose description of what you have studied.

Test scores

If you are unhappy with your initial GRE score, take the test again. Experience commonly results in a higher score. To find out about the GRE, contact the Educational Testing Service (see Appendix B, page 97). Information about the GRE can also be found at most campus career centers.

Keeping track of applications

Keep track of application forms, deadlines, and other correspondence. The worst thing about applying to graduate school is the bureaucracy. There are so many different forms that it is important to keep some kind of organized file or you will be easily overwhelmed. Keep all application materials in a manila file folder. On the inside cover, keep track of each school's requirements and your follow-up. Photocopy all materials you send out, including letters to faculty and graduate students.

Set Your Sights High

Your undergraduate professors may have commented on several graduate departments or suggested schools that might be difficult to get into, along with better prospects. After reading through your materials and assessing your interests, apply to your first choice and alternatives. By applying to several schools of varying prestige you increase your chances of acceptance. Don't sell yourself short by assuming that more eminent departments won't accept you. Women are more inclined than men to underestimate their potential worth. Try not to feel intimidated. Women should apply to departments where men of comparable qualifications are likely to be accepted. Better schools have more scholarship money, are more likely to keep their graduate classes filled, and have better placement records. Apply to as many of the better-known schools as you can, taking care to submit applications to some of the lesser-known institutions as well.

3
Graduate Study

In most MA and PhD programs, you are expected to learn an enormous amount about several loosely defined fields of history, pass a series of nightmarish exams, and then write a dissertation. There are variations on this pattern, which may be a reason to choose a certain university. It is important that you have a clear sense of what is expected of you. Graduate students often start by taking a sizable number of courses, some of which might be similar to undergraduate courses. The catch is that you are expected to approach these courses in a different way, though no one says so directly. You will absorb the material more fully than do most undergraduates and also acquire some historians' lore, such as the names and distinctive views of the leading historians who have written on the subject. As an undergraduate, you probably spent considerable time getting the facts straight; in graduate school you will spend more time exploring the range of interpretations of those facts. You will also discover different research techniques, begin to understand and practice scholarly criticism, and develop a greater command of the facts.

Fields and Subfields

You should understand the function of the program you have entered. There are basic differences between master's and PhD programs. Most master's programs involve four semesters of course work and a final master's thesis. Some programs do not require a thesis but may require additional credit hours and a written or oral examination.

PhD programs generally involve about seventy-two hours of course work, written and/or oral examinations, language requirements, and a dissertation and its defense. Requirements vary, so it is important to know what is expected of you at different phases of your graduate career.

Consult your department's guidelines on how to pick the fields in which you will concentrate. Fields of study are usually divided according to topic, region, and time period. Departments may relax some regulations if you present viable reasons, so think freely about what will be beneficial. One way to approach your field of study is to think of the subject you want to specialize in and then choose areas that fit well around it. As you begin, you might define your field as European. As you study more, you may become a modern European scholar and concentrate on labor and gender. Consult your adviser. Try to make plans early to avoid scattering your efforts, but remain receptive to new possibilities. You might develop enthusiasm for a topic that used to bore you. Overall, you should know the requirements for the fields you have chosen, including languages or field study.

Course Work

Reading or research seminars

These are virtually universal in graduate study. Research courses allow you to learn by doing. The grade is based almost entirely on a long paper, which should be the result of original research. Reading courses often require a paper analyzing what you have read, as well as discussion on those readings. Seminars are occasions for learning about methodology, bibliography, historiography, and philosophy suitable to certain fields of history. The seminar should be extremely valuable. The program probably requires you to take a small number of seminars, and you should view them as an opportunity to expand and refine your historical skills. Not only are they uniquely valuable in graduate education, but they can get you started toward publication. Intimidating though this idea may be, aim at writing a publishable article in each research seminar. You may succeed. Ask for help from your teacher. With luck and effort, you may finish your graduate work with one or two respectable articles to your credit.

Seminars also train you to behave like a historian. While researching, you absorb the folkways and values of historians and develop a sense of yourself as a professional scholar. In the discussion of research papers, which is a normal part of a research seminar, you will learn to become a responsible critic of your colleagues' work. All scholars need this give-and-take; don't think you are cruel or are betraying someone by voicing adverse judgments. At the same time, a good critic makes the effort to take seriously another's argument on its own terms. Asking someone else to write the book you'd like to have written is the easiest and often the least useful form of criticism, but it remains the most pervasive. Nasty, sarcastic, or belittling remarks are unacceptable. The most effective, intelligent criticism is always constructive.

Your teacher may present a paper, too; that has been known to happen. Treat your teacher's paper with just as much rigor, generosity, and irreverence as you would any other.

Supplementary courses in other departments

While most of your course work will be in the history department, classes offered by other departments, such as in literature, film, or sociology, will often be extremely useful in building your critical and research skills. You should also look into course offerings in interdisciplinary programs, such as women's studies and multicultural studies. Here you will find intellectual stimulation and new colleagues.

If offered the opportunity to take a course in statistical methods, do so. Even if your own work does not rely on these techniques, you will need to understand them in order to comprehend the work of other scholars.

Comprehensive Examinations

As you complete your course work, you will be ready to start thinking about taking your comprehensive exams. Examinations offer you the opportunity to sift through long periods of history and to construct your own interpretations. Whatever the form of the exam—oral, written, or both—it will seem terrifying. Other graduate students will regale you with ghastly tales of what they went through. Gathering this fund of anecdotes, scanning your patchwork of preparation, you might conclude that you ought to put off the terrible day. However, watch other successful graduate students. How long do they study? How much information seems required to pass? Ask your prospective examiners what they expect. Professors know it is easy to find out what a student does not know. Most want to find a topic a candidate can talk about intelligently, so they will probably offer you some clues in advance. Examiners will be as interested in your ability to articulate your own opinions as they are in your ability to accurately recount others' interpretations. Many students find it helpful to get together in informal study groups to prepare for examinations. You may want to start such a group. Steel yourself and set a date for your examination.

As you study for your exams, assemble bibliographies of required and supplemental readings. Go over these bibliographies with your examination committee. Discuss your interpretations of the readings. Ask members of the committee to propose questions, then talk or write through the answers.

If you have any input in selecting the faculty who will be on your examination committee, think about compatibility factors. Not only should you feel comfortable with the faculty members, but they should feel comfortable with each other, as well.

The Dissertation

Choosing a topic

Once you have passed the big exams, or even before that, you must select a dissertation topic. If possible, you want to work on a topic that fits in with current scholarship trends but also strikes out in new directions. Your dissertation topic indicates to colleagues your research and teaching interests. This choice will determine what will occupy your thoughts for the next several years and govern where you live for a while. Obviously, the subject will determine the limits of what you can say about it and the concepts you can use. You will need accessible primary sources that yield sufficient information. Scout out possibilities early. Work closely with your adviser in both choosing and developing your topic. Your adviser will help you shape an idea into a workable project. Ideally, a student's reputation is made by the dissertation. A special distinction may be accorded for thinking up an original subject. Make your own choice, rather than accepting a topic chosen by your adviser, and widen the possibilities to include a first-rate discovery rather than a humdrum rehashing or an improbable interpretation. As soon as you have chosen your topic, submit it to the American Historical Association for inclusion in its data base for *Doctoral Dissertations in History*.

Women students should take special care in choosing a subject. In some schools, some advisers still give poor guidance because they are convinced, perhaps subconsciously, that women lack creativity and will not do justice to a significant topic, or that women will not finish their dissertations. Many women graduate students have been strongly encouraged by advisers either to choose *or* to avoid work in women's history. Ignorance as well as misogyny may lie behind such advice. Women should seek help outside their departments if they detect these attitudes. Some students have written to women at other schools who have worked in their proposed field and asked for assistance. You may want to refer to the most recent edition of the AHA's *Directory of Women Historians* or its annual *Directory of History Departments and Organizations in the United States and Canada* to look for a likely adviser. Occasionally, these faculty women or other professionals have become informal mentors and have read drafts of students' work and conferred with them at conferences and other professional meetings. On your own campus, women in other departments can also provide support and encouragement. They may have helpful suggestions for on-campus mentors or study and support groups. Don't assume that just because these women are in other disciplines they will not understand your needs. The interdisciplinary nature of much scholarship fosters these relationships. Many departments now require an outside dissertation reader who is not a member of the department. Knowing faculty in other departments will help you as you form your committee.

The largest professional gathering of women historians is the Berkshire Conference on the History of Women. The "Big Berks" conference meets every three years at an Eastern college. You also will find membership in the Coordinating Committee for Women in the Historical Profession (CCWHP) to be a vital link in the world of women historians. (Other organizations are listed in Appendix B, page 97.)

Likewise, students of color often face prejudices and biases as they pursue their studies. Advisers might too readily assume that these students will automatically want to work on subjects relating to people of color for their dissertation. Students of color and lesbian and gay students may also have to go beyond their own advisers for a fresh perspective as they develop their dissertation proposal. Even if an adviser is very receptive to a student's ideas, a candidate might find more help in other departments or with outside scholarly networks.

Dissertation work can be isolating. Group support can be critical to success. Initiate a dissertation study or writing group if there is not one already in your department. Presentations of ongoing work to departmental seminars by graduate students are also a good way to build support and interest in your work, to try out ideas, and to develop confidence.

The dissertation proposal

Many departments want you to submit a plan of action on your subject, often called the dissertation proposal. The idea is to prevent students from trying impossible projects that would never win final approval. Some faculty members might even have doubts about a viable proposal, but these objections are often based on sketchy knowledge and can be overcome with more details. If opposition seems likely, plan to enlist the aid of your supervisor in pursuing tactics that will gain approval of your prospectus. You may be asked to present your plans in writing, orally, or both. Preparing the proposal will help clarify your thoughts. You want your prospectus to offer a clear research outline covering the subject you intend to pursue, how you intend to do so, and what conclusions you expect to reach. While your teachers will evaluate your past work when writing letters of recommendation for grants, your proposal is their only guide to your current course of study. Realize that there is an element of projection in the exercise. If you knew how the work would turn out, it would not be worth doing. What you forecast is only an educated guess, but it is an important guiding post. Establishing clear working hypotheses—even if you ultimately abandon or reject them—offers a way for you to get on with the initial stages of your research. The project almost surely will reshape itself as your work progresses.

Ask to see samples of successful dissertation proposals written for your department. You may find that one of the most common formats used in your department is a narrative of speculative questions that lead to the hypotheses. After looking over one or two proposals, ask the writers, if possible, whether they have turned their proposals into grant applications. There are numerous grants available for doctoral students. Ask your graduate adviser for help in locating sources and see Chapter 5, Funding Graduate and Postdoctoral Study.

Beginning the dissertation

Whatever subject you choose for a dissertation, however you get advice, you must research and write it. Speak to your adviser and clarify expectations about how you will proceed. Maintaining a good working relationship with your adviser is essential and, for good or ill, it is chiefly up to you to accommodate the relationship. Remember that your adviser, at this point, knows more than you do about writing history.

When you begin your research, you must gather and analyze the data. Procedures vary from one project to another, and yet the temptation almost always arises to keep going, to find out every last detail, to look at every conceivable source, to try all imaginable statistical devices. At some point, you have to stop gathering information and start writing. In virtually all projects the time comes when the yield from your efforts shrinks noticeably. You may not have learned all there is to learn but you have learned enough. In any case, this point of diminishing returns is the place to stop research and start composing a text. Don't feel that you have to begin at the beginning. Start with the section you feel most confident about. The introduction often will be the last thing you write.

How you present your work to your supervisor, of course, is not wholly in your control. You may be called upon to hand in chapters at regular intervals. Beware of spending your time digesting your adviser's comments and revising the parts you've already written. While you need input as you research and write, it may be better to write a first draft of the whole thing, if your adviser will be content with this procedure. Then you can revise it as a whole. *And you will revise.* But be aware that if your adviser sets different rules, you will have to comply.

Choose a dissertation topic with potential for publication as a book. Always bear in mind that a dissertation is a dissertation, and a monograph is a monograph. Virtually any dissertation will require some revision before being published as a book. When you apply for a job, it is to your advantage to have a book contract. On the other hand, producing a manuscript of this quality takes longer and requires consultation with a professional editor from a university press or commercial publisher. The AHA publishes a pamphlet, *A Guide to Book Publication for Historians,* which may prove helpful. Consider addressing this subject with members of your committee; the job market could well determine your decision.

Making progress

The dissertation is the last stage of your graduate study. Don't let it become a stumbling block. It is not wise to put off making a living forever, and it becomes demoralizing to drag out graduate school. There are also professional reasons: Potential employers

LIBRARY
EASTERN OREGON STATE COLLEGE
LA GRANDE, OR 97850

look at how long you took to complete your degree. They want an employee who gets things done.

While parents of young children, or others with exceptional circumstances, may have good reasons for taking longer than usual to get a degree, it is important to proceed efficiently. If, however, you find yourself unable to focus exclusively on your studies, don't feel as though you don't belong in the profession.

Changing Programs or Institutions

Despite the selection of the fields of study and examinations, regardless of the forethought you have given your choice, your plans may change in light of what you learn. Interests based on undergraduate experiences often fade in graduate school. It is folly to stick with a subject you once loved if it becomes unbearably dreary.

If switching fields leads to a delay in acquiring languages or other skills, you may decide against such a change. The delay can be both long and expensive if, for example, you set out to master a non-European language. These extra burdens, however, are often worth it in the long run. Consult professors and other graduate students, of course, but remember that you alone can decide what to do.

At one time or another, discouragement and doubt strike most graduate students. Don't consider your own a sign of personal weakness or failure. Joyce Antler, commenting in "Personal Lives and Professional Careers: The Uneasy Balance" (Report of the Women's Committee of the American Studies Association), found that, according to a survey conducted in 1986, one of the most frequent personal problems faced by women academics is attitudinal, "characterized by self-doubt and guilt." According to the survey, women internalized blame for their perceived failure to meet their own professional or personal goals. This is a result of the privatization of academic stress and indicates the need for many more support systems for women and men at every phase of their careers. Try not to be overly influenced by these feelings if you can avoid it, but if you do, know that you are experiencing common human reactions to stress.

If you find that you are maltreated or find one program unsuitable, another may suit you better. You may have started out, for example, as a historian but soon discovered that contemporary social problems interest you more. See an academic ad-

LIBRARY
EASTERN OREGON STATE COLLEGE
LA GRANDE, OR 97850

viser about switching departments or programs. Some credits you have accrued may be transferable. If a move is feasible, you might explore the possibility of changing universities. Such undertakings, however, whether among programs, departments, or universities, could be extremely costly. There is the risk of losing credits, and completion of the course of study may be delayed.

Leaving the Profession

There is no point in subjecting yourself to more than a year of graduate school if you do not want to spend a good deal of your life working in the field of professional history. There are no laws that you must complete a degree just because you have started one.

If you are unsure of your motives for wanting a change, take a leave of absence for a year. Try working in a field that you think offers an alternative career. A year may be all you need to reach a conclusion about where your interests and talents lie.

Professional Networking

Networking will broaden your professional horizons by exposing you to new situations and providing you with opportunities to meet historians in many different fields. It offers you a chance to look ahead into the world of historians to see how it appeals to you. If students are involved in your department's major committees, your participation may tell you a great deal about historians' values and expectations. The most educational experience is participation in a search committee's hunt for a new member of the department.

Joining scholars' associations will be helpful, too. These organizations usually offer reduced rates for students. For your dues, you will receive journals and newsletters that fill you in on new developments in scholarship and acquaint you with the current issues in the profession. These publications also announce fellowships and upcoming conferences. Some of these organizations are listed in Appendix B, page 97, but check with your adviser or mentor for other publications relevant to your field. Subscriptions to such associations' journals usually place your name on publishers' mailing lists. Publishers' catalogs will keep you abreast of new publications.

Attend departmental seminars, historical meetings in your region, and if possible, national conventions. Meetings can yield immediate and long-term rewards even if they seem intimidating at first. The scheduled panels will give you a sense of what is expected when papers are presented and will help you plan to present a paper of your own. If you are an experienced conventioneer, you are less likely to be unnerved by the frenetic atmosphere at the convention where you may have your first job interview. Seek information about which associations are most likely to include student papers on their programs.

Don't let scheduled events at conferences absorb all your energy. The unscheduled opportunities to meet and exchange notes with people whose academic interests parallel your own are important advantages of going to professional meetings. This give-and-take can be personally and intellectually rewarding and may provide opportunities to offset the shortage or absence of role models for women graduate students, students of color, and gay and lesbian students. Meetings within the larger conference bring together articulate, dedicated, friendly scholars who share your interests and professional concerns. These smaller meetings will also provide a refuge. Remember that the bigger the convention, the more hectic the atmosphere will be. Scholars are also looking for other scholars. Don't feel ignored or discouraged when your conversations are brusque or cut short. It is important to make the effort to become part of the group.

Summer Jobs, Internships, and Volunteer Work

Summer jobs, internships, and volunteer work can provide you with opportunities to test your interest in a variety of fields. Internships are available with local, state, or federal agencies; foundations; newspapers and other media organizations; public interest groups; and other professions. Some pay well. All give you a chance to develop skills not cultivated in graduate school. After completing an internship, you may decide you would rather work as a historian with a state government than teach, or perhaps you would prefer to leave the profession and become a journalist. *Careers for Students of History,* a pamphlet prepared by the American Historical Association and the National Council on Public History, covers a broad range of occupations for historians. It includes information on internships, summer and volunteer jobs, and a bibliography of publications issued by professional organizations.

Temporary jobs will give you a new perspective on academic work. They will also look good on your record when you seek long-term employment, particularly if the positions are history-related. Historic preservation work, editing, archival research, or apprenticeships at museums are all areas that indicate a serious professional interest in history and demonstrate your willingness to develop skills beyond the usual graduate school offerings. Part-time work also can provide job contacts or a lucrative way to help finance your dissertation. Most importantly, involvement in professional activities will encourage you to take yourself seriously as a scholar—perhaps the most important element for success in graduate school and professional self-definition.

4
Academic Relationships

... with Graduate Students

You will learn a great deal from other graduate students. You will meet veterans as well as beginners. You will find out what lies ahead of you, and you will learn about the unwritten rules of department life.

Graduate life should be characterized by intellectual give-and-take. Do what you can to make the company of other graduate students pleasant and intellectually rewarding by cultivating friendships with graduate students whose ideas and insights you appreciate. In addition to students in your own department, seek out students with similar interests in other departments. These people will listen to your ideas, read your papers, hear rehearsals of your public performances, offer opinions on your efforts, argue with you—and you must do the same for them—all without exposing anyone in the group to undue mental wear-and-tear. Such friendships often last a lifetime.

Opportunities exist to expand your network of graduate student colleagues throughout the United States. A number of professional organizations facilitate such interaction, including the Coordinating Committee on Women in the Historical Profession, the Association of Black Women Historians, the Berkshire Conference on the History of Women, the American Historical Association, the Organization of American Historians, and other conference groups that focus on specific areas of study. As noted earlier, joining these organizations and attending the gatherings and sessions of graduate students cannot be overemphasized.

... with Faculty

Get to know the faculty. You are planning to be a colleague someday, so it is reasonable to become familiar with faculty members. Women also may have the task of demonstrating to professors, who are usually male, their seriousness as students and their intent to someday be a professional historian and a colleague. Faculty men often have trouble seeing women on that path.

Faculty members expect more frequent dealings with graduate students than with undergraduates. See faculty members during office hours. Have your purpose clearly thought out and know how to end a conversation. You will be welcome for transactions of legitimate business and a certain amount of friendly conversation, but prolonged idle chitchat will put a strain on both of you. Do not overstay your welcome. Express your appreciation, then leave.

Some relationships with faculty will be particularly helpful to you, so pursue them. Seek out teachers who offer courses in your field. You should be able to respect them and to rely on them to recognize your successes but also to indicate your shortcomings. Faculty friends can give you personal reassurance and candid advice when needed. Often a senior woman faculty member, if this rare creature exists in the department, will be a remarkably helpful adviser to a female graduate student. But remember that faculty men may also be on your side.

Participate in seminars with faculty members from your department, other departments in the college, and with outside speakers. Interdisciplinary seminars are often open to all interested scholars at any level. Watch how academics interact with one another. Learn what is considered a good seminar presentation, a good job talk, or a publishable paper. Gain as much insight as you can by watching and interacting with faculty in these settings.

You will need a faculty supervisor or adviser, or a team of supervisors, for your main field and the writing of your dissertation. The relationship between student and adviser takes many forms, primarily determined by the personality and pedagogical methods of the adviser. No matter what the individual approach to interacting with a student, the adviser's purpose is clear: to help you choose a subject, hear about your progress, make suggestions, speak for you if you want graduate assistantships or fellowships, help you revise drafts, and start the process of advertising you for career positions. If you get anything less you are being shortchanged. If you have a choice, it is wise to choose an adviser on the basis of what you know about the person's mentoring style in this vital relationship—always taking into account other pertinent considerations, such as academic fields or department restrictions.

The recent American Studies Association survey ("Personal Lives and Professional Careers: The Uneasy Balance") indicates that women in academic positions today have trouble finding role models or mentors. A large number of women who participated in the questionnaire reported that their mentors were men. This report indicates that women graduate students should be open to mentoring from whomever is offering it—women professors, male dissertation advisers, family members, or friends. What is important is that you build a support network. Accept support when it is offered and seek it out when you feel the need for it. Some day you may be in a position to offer support to other struggling graduate students, male or female.

The Issue of Sexual Harassment

When choosing an adviser, watch out for professors who are "friendly" in ways that will interfere with your education. For women there can be distinctive hazards in this regard, but there are generic concerns as well. Teachers who want hero worship or various kinds of psychological nourishment from their students often have trouble maintaining pedagogical rigor. Friendliness, of course, comes in healthier forms, and everyone appreciates it, but you should put scholarship first in your relationship with an adviser. Unfortunately, some professors will resort to sexual innuendo and harassment. This happens more often than one might think and is *never* to be tolerated.

Tap into the student network to find out where trouble may lie. Because relatively few sexual harassers are actually prosecuted, information on potential offenders may only be available through a campus grapevine. Tread with caution here and try to determine, from people you trust, what information is considered reliable.

Victims of sexual harassment, understandably, may prefer not to publicize their experiences, which makes later victims think they have encountered something highly unusual. Confused, ashamed, or even ambivalent about their own feelings, victims may try to pretend they are misreading the signals. Difficult though it may be, analyze what is going on and take action if you have grounds for complaint. If you are confused about what is going on, confront the person directly. Often your forthright questioning will stop the offensive behavior. But if your efforts prove unavailing, *don't be passive.* Seek assistance. Ask your peers if they have ever been harassed, or if they know someone who has had similar experiences. Report the problem to your adviser, mentor, or someone you can trust. Follow up your verbal complaint in writing. The consequences of these events can be serious. It is important to think clearly and act rationally, even though such occurrences are undoubtedly disturbing.

Remember: Sexual harassment is against the law. The Supreme Court's *Meritor Savings Bank, FSB v. Vinson* decision reinforced the 1980 Guidelines issued by the Equal Employment Opportunity Commission that sexual harassment violates Section 703 of Title VII of the Civil Rights Act of 1964, and is therefore a form of sex discrimination. Unwelcome sexual advances, requests for sexual favors, and other verbal or physical conduct of a sexual nature constitute sexual harassment when it has the purpose or effect of unreasonably interfering with an individual's work performance or creates an intimidating, hostile, or offensive work environment. In an academic setting sexual harassment can be student-student, student-faculty, or employee-supervisor related. It can also come from someone of the same sex. It can affect success in a course, the opportunity to take a course, dissertation advisement, promotion, hiring, fellowships, scholarships, salary increases, letters of recommendation, and working conditions. The American Historical Association's "Statement on Standards of Professional Conduct" and the National Council on Public History's "Ethical Guidelines for the Historian" address this very serious offense.

Many schools now have grievance procedures to handle sexual harassment cases. Find out first if your department has written guidelines concerning the issue. If not, it should. If you believe that you have been sexually harassed, seek help from appropriate sources immediately. Know your rights. There are ways of dealing with harassment short of bringing a lawsuit. Let the harasser know unequivocally, in person or in writing, that the behavior is unwanted and uninvited. If you do this in writing, keep a copy and any proof that it was delivered to the harasser. Document each incident, including when and where it occurred, your response, who witnessed the incident, and whom you told. Keep these materials in a safe place (not at work). Keep a record of any letters, cards, or notes sent to you. Keep a record of your class work if relevant. Make a note of emotional or physical side effects, and document any medical consultations. Your affirmative action officer should be able to advise you while keeping your identity confidential. File a formal complaint if your department or college has an internal complaint system. If this does not work, contact an attorney experienced in handling sexual harassment cases and begin to work through outside channels. Along with these actions, seek personal support. Contact a professional counselor. Ask for a referral from a friend, a local clinic, or call a help hotline. Many campuses and communities fund such local resources.

The Returning Student

As an adult student, you have a more defined sense of self and are accustomed to a career and/or family life. Entering graduate school may have a different meaning for you than it has for younger peers. It is impossible to ignore family and other responsibilities in order to spend more time at a library or to do some last-minute work on a paper. A marked drop in your standard of living will follow if you give up a salary for graduate study.

Watch out for possible consequences of being out of the usual sequence in higher education. For example, women and men who enter graduate schools directly after college arrive with study habits that you probably have long since discarded. Your priorities will shift as you make progress toward your degree. The first years of course work require organized commitments, often with little flexibility, and are followed by examinations and writing the dissertation—which allows you more independence in creating a schedule. It should get easier as you move toward your degree. Instead of seeing graduate work as one long continuing process, focus on it as a series of phases that will present different obligations and freedoms. The early years may be rigorously scheduled, but the expectations—attendance at classes and completion of papers—are clearly drawn. The later years provide flexibility but also require the ability to work independently.

Teachers are accustomed to students who exhibit typical student reflexes and outlooks. Instructors are sometimes younger than adult students and may treat you like other students, which can be disconcerting. The instructor's behavior may not be intentionally condescending, but it may appear that way to someone who has "lived in the adult world," and resentment may develop, taking the form of objecting to assignments or degree requirements. Beware of this psychological trap. Examine the situation objectively. Look for other faculty or students who can offer a better perspective on the situation. Above all, avoid convincing yourself that the parts of graduate training that you find irksome or inconvenient are simply obnoxious impositions. From time to time every department reviews its rules to adjust to changing realities, and the returning student can bring a fresh perspective to the process. Naturally, teachers find it easier to treat everyone alike rather than to develop a plan of study for each student. However, within the parameters of a sound education, teachers should tailor study to the student. A dialogue between older students and teachers may be a simple and direct solution.

Be careful, however, of asking for exemption from the usual rules on the grounds that your goals are different from those of other students. You may have limited aspirations at the outset, but you may change your mind later and will want the same treatment—perhaps in job placement—everyone else receives. If you have bypassed a particular requirement, your professors will have some doubts about how to evaluate you. For example, you may initially only want to satisfy an intellectual curiosity in a defined field and consequently may regard a required historiography or quantitative methods course as an arbitrary hurdle. If you successfully petition for a waiver on this requirement, then develop ambitions for professional employment, you should not expect to be recommended along with those who have followed the plan of study established by the department.

Academic relationships are complex and constantly changing. The intellectual stimulation of a study group, the rewards of a good student-mentor relationship, the shared hopes and insights of students of all ages and backgrounds pursuing the common goals of higher education—these are the connections that foster growth and progress. Academic relationships are the foundation and support structures of building a professional career.

5
Funding Graduate and Postdoctoral Study

Many graduate students receive funding to help pay for all or part of their graduate education. In the best of cases, funding covers every year of course work for the MA or PhD and the dissertation stage. Funding is also available for postdoctoral study. Rarely, though, does all such funding come from the same source. It is important that you know both the phases of funding and how to apply for it.

Graduate Assistantships

During your graduate study, it is possible your department will offer you part-time employment, whether in research, administration, or teaching. This offer may be made when you are first accepted into a program but more likely will come in your second or third year. The titles differ: graduate assistant, research associate, teaching fellow, half-time lecturer, among others. Be sure you know what duties you will be expected to perform. All assistantships should be paid, have a stipulated number of hours per week, and a predetermined work schedule for the semester. When you know the particulars you can decide whether you want the job.

Pay for an assistantship will be meager. Everyone bemoans how low it is; nobody raises it much except to offset inflation. You may want to agitate for higher pay. If so, you have a strong claim. There are campuses where graduate students have attempted to unionize, drawing on relationships with other staff unions. You might want to explore this possibility, although initially, at least, you will have enough to do without adding on the responsibilities of unionizing.

If you want an assistantship, apply early. Keep careful track of deadlines for applications and renewals. Your adviser should have up-to-date knowledge of your progress and will generally act as an advocate on your behalf to the assistantship committee. Normally, your adviser can manage the campaign without your doing much, but you may find it useful to know how the assistantships are awarded. This depends on the size of the department and its resources. Your adviser may not be around for the final decision. In general, you will be judged on your successful graduate study and your aptitude for the work ahead.

Teaching assistantships

Teaching assistantships are designed to provide you with teaching skills. Like an apprenticeship, this affords you an opportunity to learn under professional guidance. Supervision decreases as your teaching experience increases. You often gain experience in courses outside your particular field. Most permanent teaching positions will require you to teach survey courses, and these will need preparation. All teaching assistants are evaluated by both students and professors; their judgments will help you learn and, when the reports are good, will help you get a full-time job.

When you work as a TA in a course conducted by a full-time faculty member, that person is in charge of your professional conduct in that course. Therefore, that teacher may stipulate the assignments for your students in whole or in part; visit your classes; call on you to explain grades you assign or change them; or ask you to exchange papers for grading with another section assistant. The skillful supervisor will track your responsibilities, consult with you about improving the course, and conduct staff meetings where administrative details are cleared up quickly and the subject of the course is discussed.

Success as a teaching assistant can be extremely valuable when you look for a full-time teaching position. Everyone looks for evidence of pedagogical skills in candidates. It is greatly in your interest, therefore, to do well and to have faculty observers witness your triumphs in the classroom. Their comments, supported by student evaluations, will carry great weight. Still, being a TA has diminishing returns, especially if you are still only assisting in large survey courses. It is important to pursue opportunities to structure your own courses. And, if you have the choice between a teaching assistantship and a fellowship, you should remember that teaching always takes a great deal of time and can keep you from completing your dissertation.

Research assistantships

Research assistantships generally vary from teaching assistantships in that they build different skills and sometimes allow for more flexible work schedules. Students interested in public history jobs may prefer research assistantships. Their required tasks may range from working as a data gatherer and editor on a manuscript to data accumulation and cataloging for an archive. If possible, pursue a research assistantship at least once in your graduate years to help you build these practical historical skills.

Fellowships and Grants

Departments and colleges are not the only sources of funding for graduate studies, so do not rely solely on them for all your financial needs. As you move into the dissertation phase, begin gathering information about other funding sources. This section focuses on the process of applying for fellowships and grants. In some cases, fellowships or grants can be used to supplement department assistantships. MA students will also find information of interest.

There are many fellowships specifically targeted to graduate students. However, graduate students should consider themselves eligible for any grant directed at historical scholarship unless the granting agency specifically targets another audience (such as holders of the PhD) or indicates that graduate students are not eligible. While competition may be greater for these grants, they are not unattainable.

A Word about Committee Decisions

The committees that award fellowships tend to be chosen from the disciplinary establishment and to recognize merit in those with similar characteristics and interests. Without malicious intent, such committees also try to reduce risk. Painfully conscious of how little money there is to distribute, they put great weight on the reliability of references and proof of productivity. Nonetheless, foundations have been increasingly aware of the need to diversify, and some organizations have been more sensitive than others to the needs of aspiring scholars. A well-written application for a strong project can win a fellowship based on merit *and* strategy.

Preliminary inquiries

Ask friends and former teachers about agencies to approach. Check out fellowship directories, such as the AHA's annual publication, *Grants, Fellowships, & Prizes of Interest to Historians*.

Many universities now have a grants officer, whose duty it is to help faculty members write proposals for outside grants and fellowships. A grants officer will have material on hand from most funding agencies—application forms, statements of purpose, and the like—and experience in dealing with such agencies. The grants officer can help in many ways—such as calling the agency to clarify a question, or reading and commenting on your proposal. Don't assume, however, that the grants officer will know of all grants available to you. While grants officers attempt to be thorough, they also are usually responsible for covering many disciplines and may not be fully informed about all grants available to historians. If no such position exists at your university, you must go through the preliminary inquiries yourself.

If you are not sure if your project or qualifications will be judged suitable by a particular agency, write and ask. If there is any hint of requirements that would prejudice or prevent application because of race, sex, or age, press the agency further and notify the AHA of the suspected discrimination at once.

When you write to an agency for an application, also ask for annual reports of the organization and the list of awards for the past several years. These can give you important clues that are not always specified in the fellowship brochure. The agency's policies can change as scholarly fields shift and as administrators come and go. The organization may concentrate grants regionally or prefer certain subjects or research methods. If such policies exist and suit you, fine. If not, write to find out if certain policies rule out your project. You may be saved the bother of applying.

Filing the application

Be sure to fill out the application form neatly and precisely. Stay within the recommended length, remembering that fellowship committees often have to read hundreds of applications. If you can, follow the style of a successful application; it can provide a helpful model. Some agencies accept preliminary proposals. If so, take advantage of this opportunity of help from agency staff.

Recognize your weaknesses as far as the agency is concerned, and emphasize your strengths on the application. Women in general, and older women especially, ought to emphasize their professional attitudes and commitment. This is best done not by direct assertion but by tone and statement of career plans. If your career shows unusual gaps that require explanation, like a period of withdrawal for family responsibilities or a paucity of research due to heavy teaching responsibilities, make a brief, straightforward statement of the facts with no apologies.

Choose people to write letters of recommendation or to referee your proposal who will strengthen your position. It is always wise to choose people who are clearly your senior in the field. If you are working in a subject that requires a variety of skills, try to get people who can testify to all needed attributes. If your career has been limited to a particular locale or to a wholly teaching-oriented institution, try to include a recommendation from someone in a nationally recognized department, even if that person is only familiar with an earlier stage of your career. It is almost always useful to get letters of recommendation from people outside your home institution.

If submission of supporting materials is permitted, these may be helpful, but don't send very long papers. If you must, add an abstract indicating which sections show the heart of your work.

If a budget is required as part of the application, be as realistic as possible in estimating your needs. As important as the total amount of money requested is the rationale, so add a note explaining your reasoning in constructing the budget. Agencies differ on such requirements, and it is wise to seek the advice of someone who is well informed about a particular agency.

The project statement

Your statement of the project should be oriented to each individual agency. Most subjects have many dimensions, and it is entirely appropriate to emphasize the area in which each agency is particularly interested. For example, if you want to write a biography of Elizabeth Blackwell, you might stress to the Rockefeller Program in Women's Studies how your book will add to the understanding of women in the nineteenth century; to the National Institutes of Health Program in the History of Medicine you can relate your study to the history of medical practice; to the Social Science Research Council you can show how Blackwell illuminates problems of professionalization and gender roles; to the National Endowment for the Humanities you might emphasize the variety of topics Blackwell's life and work spanned and your intent to relate her accomplishments to a wider audience. You cannot, of course, claim to do all these things unless you really intend to. But the process of applying for fellowships should lead you to discover the richness of your own subject and to think systematically about how to bring it out.

Your project statement should focus on the questions and issues it addresses, not on a narrative statement of the subject. A biography, for instance, is a traditional form that in itself would hold little appeal for fellowship agencies. Yet a biography can be presented—as it should be conceived—as a case study in various historical problems. This also applies to other topics. Any subject gains interest from a sharp focus on relevant historical issues.

This focus will help you make the strongest possible case for your project's importance. Even if such a statement is not required, be sure to show how your project adds to what is already known, explores new methods, or makes new materials available.

Finally, it is very important to have several other people read your proposal before you submit it. Someone well versed in your field can make useful suggestions. So can a person outside the field; things that seem clear to members of the field can mystify others. Some agencies ask you to send the proposal to a referee who then comments on the project as well as your capabilities. In that case, send it to the referee well in advance of the deadline. In addition to asking for a judgment on a recommendation, ask how the proposal might be improved. In general, be sure someone well-informed looks over the completed application, including budget and career statements as well as the prospectus of your project. Exchanging information and advice is a professional duty. Don't hesitate to ask for help.

Follow-up

If you fail to get the fellowship, do not be content with a form letter of rejection. Write and ask for advice and particulars; would it be worthwhile to apply again next year? Is there a weakness in the application that you might strengthen? Private foundations may not respond, but government agencies are now required to summarize evaluations for those who request it. Don't give up after one year's try. Many chance circumstances enter into a decision and you could succeed next time.

Assistantships, grants, and fellowships provide more than financial support. They also give you and your projects prestige. Use these awards as building blocks to more grants or jobs. Their long-term benefits are as important as their short-term rewards of skills and money.

6
The Job Search

Defining Goals

It's time to initiate your first real job search. In the 1990s, job prospects for historians look good because of an anticipated increase in retirements in academe. Many new jobs are being created, though the number of positions open at any one time also reflects the increased lateral movement of already-established historians. Nevertheless, you must approach the job market with a positive attitude and with the skills to land a good position.

Be realistic about your prospects. With a master's degree fewer doors are open to you, unless the degree is in a speciality that does not require additional study. For most professional positions the doctorate is needed, so do not pursue such positions until the PhD is clearly in sight. A certificate in special programs, such as women's history, ethnic studies, critical studies, African-American history, or public history will show prospective employers that you have specific training for certain jobs.

Be wary of financial pressures that may lead you to rush into a job. You may find that finishing a dissertation while otherwise employed takes longer than your employer is willing to wait. Even if you finish the dissertation and are able to keep your job for a few more years, you may not be able to put the effort into publishing sufficiently to qualify for a longer term. In institutions following American Association of University Professors (AAUP) guidelines, faculty members are allowed six years to qualify for tenure. That may sound like a long time, but it will pass quickly under the demands of teaching and publishers' deadlines.

Career and Placement Office Services

Your graduate school almost surely has a placement office that receives inquiries and sends basic information about candidates to prospective employers. Students usually attend orientation seminars and schedule individual appointments with a career counselor. Career counselors assist students by developing individualized career plans, discussing career alternatives, refining job-seeking skills, and providing job placement assistance. Don't assume that you must stay in the academic world as a professor. There are many other opportunities with museums and historical societies, for example, that you should consider. The career office will help you look into these possibilities.

After you have determined the kinds of jobs you want to apply for, the most important service of the career office is its credentials service. Students' academic and professional recommendations are kept on file and may be used for employment, admissions, and postgraduate fellowship purposes. Visit your placement office early and often to find out about funding and job opportunities.

The placement office should have all the appropriate forms. Your file or dossier should contain a transcript of your graduate school grades, a curriculum vitae (c.v.) or résumé on a form used by the placement office, and testimonial letters.

The Professional Dossier

The purpose of your c.v. is to show the extent of your training and experience in the historical profession. It should include basic information: name, address, telephone numbers (be sure to include both home and office numbers), and citizenship.

While you can simply photocopy your c.v. or run off a copy on a computer, using a high-quality white or ivory rag or bond paper looks more professional. A good source of information on résumé writing for historians is available from the Organization of American Historians, *From Job Crisis to Job Opportunities: The OAH/FIPSE Project Careers Packet* (see Bibliography, page 103). After listing the basic information, detail your professional education. List all degrees from BA on, but go into detail only on graduate study: fields, subject, dissertation supervisor, and other major research projects. List any honors and fellowships. Mention teaching assistantships or comparable preparation for employment.

List professional positions, most recent first, beginning with your current job. Give titles and stipulate whether the jobs were part- or full-time. Opinions differ on whether to account for gaps in employment or education. Some prefer to leave them unexplained and let prospective employers ask about them. Women or men who have interrupted a career to raise a family may want to mention it in the dossier or in the accompanying cover letter. Regardless of how you treat any gaps, make clear how you kept your professional skills polished during these intervals—by keeping abreast of publications, writing articles, attending professional meetings, and so forth.

Next, list your publications and public presentations of papers and commentary. The further you are in your career the more selective you can get. Beginners are wise to note anything that shows active participation in the profession.

Describe the work you are prepared to do—what subjects you are ready to teach or what other tasks you are trained for. A syllabus backs this up. Give a brief description of your current research, how you are revising your dissertation, and maybe a prediction of what you might work on next. If you anticipate further training, mention that.

Keep dossiers up-to-date and always have a supply of copies of your c.v. available. As your experiences accumulate, revise the basic c.v. to include your progress. Drop references that pertain only to your earliest years in graduate study and add letters from people who have a fresh understanding of your work. A common error is leaving in an outdated letter. For instance, when you have completed your dissertation, ask your adviser to write a new letter that fully evaluates what you've accomplished.

Where to Find Job Listings

Once you have decided on the positions you would like to pursue and assessed your skills, use every possible avenue to track down employment opportunities. To search for a job, turn to teachers, the department's placement officer, the college placement office, professional journal and newspaper ads, and your own initiative. For teaching positions, consult the Employment Information Bulletin (EIB), which is part of the AHA's monthly newsletter, *Perspectives;* the *Chronicle of Higher Education,* published weekly; and selected publications in your field. The *Affirmative Action Register* is directed at women, minorities, veterans, and the physically disabled and should be consulted for administrative, managerial, and professional positions. Interdisciplinary listings can be found in the *American Studies Association Newsletter.* (See Bibliography, page 103.) Some departments receive subscriptions to these publications. If your department does not, urge the administrator to sign up.

Museums are increasingly seeking historians with PhDs, so do not rule out these positions. If you want to consider this option, you may wish to do an internship in a museum, take the opportunity to consult on developing a museum exhibit, or get involved in state humanities programming; any of these activities will help you to understand for the challenges of presenting history to a broad public audience. For museum jobs, see *Aviso*, published by the American Association of Museums, and the newsletter of the American Association for State and Local History (AASLH). (See Appendix B, page 97, for addresses.)

Jobs for Public Historians

Much of the information regarding employment in colleges and universities is relevant to historians working in museums, archives, government, or state and local historical societies. However, because these positions are located in more diverse institutions, it is essential to become familiar with the structure and policies of your institution. State and federal agencies operate under civil service rules for retention and promotion. In private agencies, the board of directors may be the ultimate arbiter of hiring, evaluation, and promotion practices. In some cases, public programs or your own salary may depend on your ability to raise funds.

Public historians have the ability to reach new audiences with historical work and to educate general audiences in historical inquiry and methods. By maintaining an active presence at professional meetings, public historians can do much to educate their colleagues about the promotion of historical knowledge in this larger field. By pursuing their own scholarship and enlisting academic historians as consultants and colleagues, public historians can counter the insularity that sometimes plagues their own agencies.

For public history positions, consult publications of other professional associations in addition to *Perspectives'* EIB. If you are in an archival training program, see *American Archivist,* published by the Society of American Archivists, and consult the *S.A.A. Newsletter.*

Jobs with the Federal Government

The federal government provides many opportunities for those seeking public history employment. Federal agencies frequently have their own historical programs; the Department of Defense, for example, has a particularly large staff of military historians. The National Archives and the National Park Service are also major employers of historians, and there are many historians at the State Department.

Unfortunately, there is no reliable central source of information concerning openings for federal jobs. Each federal agency has its own personnel office (sometimes more than one) and you will need to contact each agency individually. A look at the *Government Organization Manual* will help you choose the agencies or committees where you might like to work. The AHA, the Society for History in the Federal Government, and the National Coordinating Committee for the Promotion of History jointly publish the *Directory of Federal Historical Programs and Activities,* a listing of federal offices with historians, which is available from the AHA. If you are interested in a particular department, contact that agency's staff historian. *Federal Career Guides,* published by the Federal Research Service, Inc., contains listings of federal jobs, and is available in most libraries or by subscription. Federal agencies also advertise in regular vehicles such as the *Perspectives'* EIB or in the *Chronicle of Higher Education.* For positions in the nation's capital, see the *Washington Post* classifieds.

The Dreaded SF-171

Application requirements vary for federal jobs, but you should nevertheless fill out a federal application form, known as the SF-171. It is an exhaustive form and is available from the personnel office of any federal agency or from the post office. Leave blank the sections that pertain to specific jobs, as it is permissible to submit photocopies of SF-171 forms. The most recent employment box also can be left blank, so that you can tailor your experience to highlight the features most relevant to the specific job application. In describing your experience, use the precise words or phrases that the job description includes. The person who initially screens applications may not know much—or anything—about this particular job or field and will rely on those clues in selecting eligible applicants.

The SF-171 is essentially a skills-oriented résumé, and you must explain your qualifications in terms that will make sense to someone who is not familiar with the language of scholarly credentials. Include a list of your published work and explain the research and writing skills that they demonstrate. For example, "conducted original historical research in diaries, letters, and city directories; drafted and revised essay accepted for publication on recommendation of anonymous scholarly reviewers."

Some federal job descriptions list numbered "selective factors" and "quality ranking factors" in listing the credentials required for the job. You should respond to each one by number, again very specifically. Often these overlap, but be sure to answer completely nonetheless. You are addressing two different audiences. "Selective factors" guide personnel approval for that grade and position—without such approval the search committee cannot consider your application. "Quality ranking factors" guide the search committee in their ranking of candidates from the pool approved for the position.

In addition to sending your SF-171 directly to agencies that have jobs available, you should also send one to the resident historian of the departments you are interested in, along with a c.v. and cover letter, and at least one copy to the Office of Personnel Management. Staff at OPM may subsequently send your form to agencies looking for applicants. Contact OPM for its current regulations for applying for professional positions. It may not be a bad idea to include a copy of your c.v. with the SF-171, but never send the c.v. alone.

Looking for a job with a congressional office requires a strategy different from that of an executive branch search. Keep in mind that these jobs are often very insecure, very demanding, highly competitive, and not very well paid. They can also be very exciting. Personal contacts are the first line of attack—if you know someone who works for Congress, start networking. Plainly, an "in" with your own representative is useful. Work you may have done for candidates in previous elections should provide names of people to call as well.

Try not to be unduly influenced by discouragement from your advisers. Their ideas about who's right for a job may or may not correspond to the ideas of search committees. Do not forget that you may be competing for positions with friends you've made in graduate school. Be honest in acknowledging the difficulty of this situation. Good will on all sides will make the situation easier.

A final note regarding job searches in any sector, public or private: If you know that you would not take a certain job, because of its location or for another reason, drop it from your list. Don't apply for jobs you are not ready to consider seriously. However, give yourself a fair chance—a situation may look more attractive once you've seen it close up.

7
Survival at Interviews

Successful Interviewing

The following discussion is directed both to interviewers and candidates and rests on the assumption that these two parties need not have adversarial interests. Ideally, both want to exchange as much accurate and relevant information as possible about the qualities and credentials of the candidate and the nature of the job. Yet both face temptations that can lead to unproductive interviews. One temptation for the interviewer is created by the fact that the interview often constitutes an occasion for conversing with colleagues; these occasions are unfortunately rare, especially in big departments. It is always satisfying to discover how interesting our department colleagues are, but such discussions unfortunately detract from the interview process. A related problem arises when interviewers want to demonstrate their own erudition. Interviewees frequently face the problem that their anxiety and desire not to offend may make them suppress their natural personality and appear less interesting than they actually are. Thorough planning and preparation for the interview will make such mistakes less likely.

Inadequate preparation on both sides is a very common mistake and is often the result of denial that good interviewing requires a lot of work on both sides. If the interviewer does not know the candidate's work, revealing questions may not emerge until the candidate has left. Candidates should not hesitate to send ahead any reasonable amount of material, even beyond what is requested, to strengthen their case: the goal is to make one's work known.

Unfortunately, candidates must also be prepared to face search committees who have not read this material and to present condensed descriptions of their work to other department members who may not have even read the accompanying c.v. Candidates can try to refocus a wandering interview by emphasizing their recent work.

Candidates should also study a prospective department's make-up. Are women and minorities well represented? Do faculty members represent more than one age group? What are the areas of strength and research interests among the faculty? Interviewers reasonably interpret this knowledge or lack of it as evidence of interest and sophistication.

Convention interviews

Interviews conducted at conventions are grueling situations for everyone, because many people are seen very briefly. It should be the goal of the interview to illuminate what is unique about each candidate, but to do this both sides must necessarily repeat themselves. The candidate should be able to provide capsule summaries of the dissertation or other current work, preferably in two versions: one in less than five minutes, one a bit longer. Each version should begin with a summary of main arguments (not just a description of the topic) and should at least hint at, if not cover, sources, theoretical content, and what is new and important about the work. Women in particular, but many men, too, have difficulty in asserting the importance of their work, and construe their research in the most insignificant terms possible. Avoid beginning the summary apologetically or negatively by describing what is omitted or what the work does not do. Do not be so cautious that you refuse to think and talk beyond the limits of the dissertation. Be prepared to talk about how your work will or should influence future scholarship in various areas. Be prepared to answer the question, "So what?"

Interviewers will find it useful to draw out the candidates' views of their dissertations, in order to get an opportunity to see how candidates handle a historical argument and what relationships exist between conclusion and evidence; these are tests of the candidates' qualities of mind. Interviewers often ask candidates for perspectives on the general development of the field (say, colonial U.S. history) in the past decade or two: Can candidates identify the big historiographical patterns? Do they know the literature outside their dissertation topic?

Candidates should be prepared to discuss a long-term research agenda—if possible, a project beyond the dissertation—at a minimum, a vision of how the dissertation will be revised. Candidates should consider carefully whether to present themselves as continuing the same topic or ranging further. If this question is not posed, find ways of introducing it. Again, women in particular have difficulty with setting the agenda and seizing the conversational initiative. Bolster your courage in advance, perhaps by asking friends to participate in a mock interview by posing some difficult questions.

Although the hierarchical nature of academia, and its persistent sexism in particular, may seem to provoke attitudes of deference, such behavior does not usually produce good interviews. Confidence is almost always an asset; if it isn't, maybe the job wouldn't be tolerable. This does not mean bragging or listing all your honors; real confidence is reflected in a willingness to offer genuine opinions and to respond to thought-provoking questions.

Preparing for on-campus interviews

The more carefully planned, the better the campus visit. Search committee chairs should have detailed schedules, preferably in writing, for candidates' visits. These should include rest breaks. It is helpful to find guest rooms as near as possible to the center of activity so that candidates can retire for an hour if they like. Because junior candidates may find it difficult to ask assertive questions, interviewers should provide information about the schedule and procedure for hiring decisions, how many candidates are being interviewed, and what the prospects and requirements are for tenure. Interviewers should keep questions exclusively to professional matters, and should, whenever possible, include women and minority faculty among the interviewers.

The candidates in turn should ask for detailed information about the interview procedure. Don't hesitate to ask very specific questions: What will the schedule be like (hour by hour if possible)? Where will you stay overnight? Whom will you see? If you are giving a talk, ask the size of the audience, the type of room, the make-up of the audience (whether it will be largely students, largely faculty, or open to the public), and exactly how long the talk is expected to be.

Candidates should beware of the following: Many interviewers try to set candidates at ease by emphasizing the informality of the interview. Take these assurances with a great deal of salt. You are better off sticking to generally observed formalities. This means, for example, that if a talk is expected, bring a written paper, even if you do not actually read it word for word. (The notion that people perform better when talking informally from notes is usually a myth—most people perform better with a written text that they know very well and can deviate from without collapse.) Of course, the degree of formality may vary from place to place; question your hosts closely.

49

Be very certain that your talk is the right length, the right volume, and is delivered with minimal repetitive mannerisms. If possible, practice in front of friends. Be prepared to answer any questions concisely.

Above all, present your strongest possible paper, even if recently published. See that your paper hits all the scholarly requirements—particularly a clear argument, good use of (preferably original) sources, critical standards of evidence, awareness of other relevant scholarship (particularly that written by members of the department), and is an inherently interesting and, if possible, important topic.

The specifics of a dress code are more problematic for women than for men, but they can be exaggerated. Academics in general (at least outside New York, and with other striking exceptions) are not as sensitive to fashion as many other professionals. It is appropriate to think "conservative." But it does not appear to be necessary, at least in academia, to dress like a Wall Street broker. Depending on the institution or the geographic region, a suit may not be necessary. Women might consider glancing at *Working Woman* or other magazines aimed at professional women for alternatives to "traditional" business suits. Be prepared to walk, as the distances across campuses can be great.

Once on campus, candidates are likely to have a series of brief meetings with individuals and small groups of faculty that will require repetitive descriptions of work and background. There will often be an interview with a dean. Be prepared to discuss the particulars of each section of your dissertation: research problems and how you solved them, new sources discovered, and anecdotes from within the dissertation.

Now is the time to ask questions about the department and campus. Think about this in advance so as not merely to repeat the basics. Candidates should certainly inquire about the following: teaching load, research support, leave time, enrollments, promotion and evaluation procedures, department structure, anticipated hiring, and library facilities. Try to ask about basic issues and problems that all colleges have: Is the school well funded, are salary increases made regularly, is the department congenial or factionalized, is there much interdisciplinary work for students or faculty, among other questions. It is also useful to ask about the community—its resources, schools if you have children, housing, etc. These questions can be asked without overconfidence (as if you were certain of getting the job offer).

(Appendix A: "A Checklist of Job Interview Queries," page 93, covers a broad range of pertinent issues.)

Women and minorities should direct special energy toward other women and minorities in the department. Their state of mind may tell you about conditions for women and minorities at this campus, although you should consider asking the interviewer directly about the numbers and status of women and minorities on the faculty. Candidates who ignore female and minority faculty do so at their peril. The fact that women and minorities have a harder time getting jobs and promotions does not mean they're not respected once in faculty positions, and their opinions may count for a lot.

Evidence suggests that the situation of gays and lesbians is probably not parallel. Unfortunately, if you need to get a job, identifying your sexual preference may hinder your chances for employment—unless you are absolutely certain of your reception.

Whether or not you are the top candidate, you may find the chair or someone else drawing you into a practical discussion about your interest in this job and your requirements. Do not be misled—the same discussion may be had with all interviewees. Don't hesitate to ask about what the job offer might include, but this is not a good time to make special demands that might accord you privileges above other department members, such as a lower teaching load or leave time. If you have other interviews, be sure to let them know this, but do not exaggerate.

You may also be a participant in many social occasions from breakfast through evening cocktails. Don't be fooled: These are never simply social occasions; you are always being interviewed. You might wish to avoid drinking alcohol. Interviewers may use these occasions to fish for information about your personal or family circumstances. Feel free to discuss your situation if you like, but plan your responses in advance if you wish to retain your privacy. You might respond to an inquiry on marital status by saying, "I don't have any commitments that would prevent me from taking this job." On the other hand, don't feel that you must converse only about professional topics; it is useful to let people know your other interests in life. At any time, don't hesitate to ask for small breaks (before your talk or between appointments) or to retire if you feel exhausted and need to go to sleep early. Interviewers often empathize with the strain and should be expected to sympathize with your need for a break or rest.

Women, people of color, and gay and lesbian candidates may be asked inappropriate questions or be offered barbed comments. To these there is never a simple response. Interviewers have a reasonable desire to assess a person as a potential colleague, and it is often useful to begin by giving the interviewers the benefit of the doubt by interpreting personal questions or compliments on your appearance as charitably as possible. A useful device is often silence. Give yourself time to think, and the questioner time to reflect or change the subject. If there is an implied insult, you may feel the need to challenge it directly; but if you want the job, try to help the interviewer save face. If someone compliments you on your looks, you can assume the remark was meant as a compliment, acknowledge it with a smile or a nod, and change the subject. If that fails you can respond that you understand the remark was meant kindly, but you would feel more comfortable concentrating on your academic credentials. To an inappropriate question you can respond that while you know the questioner didn't intend it, the question could be interpreted as biased so you'd just as soon skip it. This is always a difficult choice; those who make such comments are likely to receive such responses with hostility. It sometimes makes sense to swallow your sense of justice and tell the interviewer what he or she wants to hear. The best solution, of course, is for interviewers to stick to academic matters. The interview process is stressful for both parties; you or the interviewer may be more sensitive to questions or comments you deem inappropriate when no offense was meant.

No amount of good advice can obviate the fact that interviews are full of arbitrary, capricious interactions and unexpected events. Interviewees will make mistakes and a good interviewer can distinguish them from incompetence, so you need not think you must be perfect. Moreover, some of the best interviews will deviate from the rules and will exhibit some human oddities but will still honor the spirit and purpose of the event: to focus on the academic skills of the candidate.

Other Tips for Academic Interviews

Prior to a convention interview, the hiring institution should announce job specifications as clearly as possible, and also should announce ways to locate the interviewers at the convention. At large conventions such as the American Historical Association's annual meeting, recruiters often are not assigned hotel rooms in advance of registration and the efficiency of mail and phone message systems varies from hotel to hotel. Candidates sometimes have problems finding interviewers who have issued specific invitations. Therefore, interviewers at conventions should enter their names and hotel numbers as soon as possible in the locator file at convention registration.

There is conflicting opinion about whether or not to attend a convention without a prescheduled interview. If you think it will be worthwhile, go ahead. Remember, though, that you will be responsible for all your expenses for the trip, and the money might be better spent pursuing job possibilities in other ways.

Graduate students often sit on search committees. The student's status is not necessarily announced. Find out if one of the interviewers is a graduate student, then follow up with specific questions or comments about matters of concern to graduate students at the university. If graduate students from the department are not on the search committee, they may still be attending the conference, so arrangements may be made for a separate meeting. Use the locator file to set up a time to meet. This may be a good way to find out about the graduate students' views of the department.

A host department will usually reimburse your expenses for visiting the campus; but whatever the arrangements, be sure they are clear in advance. Some institutions offer little or no financial help to candidates for interviews. Such institutions may invite a large number of applicants for campus visits. On the whole, if the interview is to be mostly at your expense, your chances of getting the job are diminished. In the better case, when your way will be paid, you will be expected to provide receipts for all major expenditures. Supply your social security number; quite a few schools need it before they can reimburse you. Normally schools will reimburse you later, rather than pay for your transportation in advance.

After the interview, you have another opportunity to contact the interviewers: make sure you thank them immediately. Within a day or two of your meeting, send a letter to the chair of the search committee and to the graduate students if a separate meeting was arranged. Use appropriate business style and high-quality paper. This is your chance to emphasize or expand on how you are extremely qualified for the job and how the department would benefit by hiring you. Thank the interviewer for spending time with you.

Interviewing at Archives, Historical Societies, and Museums

The rituals and routines of professional hiring off-campus are less codified than interviews for faculty positions, but the basic objectives are similar. The interviewers want to get to know you and your abilities, and you want to know more about the prospective position and work environment. Be aware that interviewers may perceive university-based historians as somewhat insular; therefore you should show that you have thought about the special demands and rewards of doing historical work that reaches beyond a scholarly audience. Interviewers are likely to be looking for someone with a genuine interest in their constituency, be that the museum-going public, the research-oriented clientele of an archives, or the supporting agency itself, as in the U.S. Senate Historical Office or the Federal Judicial Center. Find out about the structure and funding of the institution and its projects.

Interviewees should be aware that the daily routines, expectations, and resources of such positions vary greatly. In a small museum with a modest budget, you may be responsible for raising money, planning programs, and designing and hanging exhibits, as well as providing historical expertise. In a large agency, you may carry out specific duties on a daily basis and also get the opportunity to initiate your own special projects. You should ask about issues such as travel money, support for research, leave time, and the like. Some positions offer little or no time for individual research; others consider such work an integral part of professional advancement. At the same time, beware of focusing only on the prerequisites. Just as university search committees would look askance at a candidate who appeared uninterested in teaching, so, too, are museums, archives, and agencies reluctant to hire someone who may want only to be seen as a future scholar-in-residence. You must focus on how your skills and interests fit the central work of the institution.

Awaiting a Response

When you leave an interview, the interviewers usually thank you for your time and say they have learned a lot from talking with you. Don't expect to be offered a job on the spot. Only in the rarest occasions does this happen.

Most interviewers will inform you when they have made a selection, but practice differs as to when the word will be sent. Some schools will tell you as soon as they have taken you off the list. That ends the suspense and many candidates are grateful for the small relief. Other schools think it kinder to say nothing until they have made an offer that has been accepted or until the search has been given up for some reason. A letter reporting the result is then sent to all who have been interested in the position. This procedure avoids offending those who have been ruled out early. It assures the candidates that the position actually has been filled, abolished, or may be filled after a further search. Candidates should feel free to ask for reasons why they were taken off the list. Keep in mind, though, that the answers may be less than satisfactory because they are phrased to avoid giving occasion for further inquiry or lawsuit; however, they may be helpful guides for future interviews. Candidates should also feel free to ask for immediate notification if they are eliminated from the list of prospects and should expect some kind of word sooner or later. Above all, anyone who has been invited for an on-campus interview and then removed from the list has a right to hear about the decision. Rejection is not easy, but there are other issues at stake besides you and your qualifications. A department hires around its current weaknesses and to build on its strengths. Also, new PhDs should be aware that they are in competition with people who have more experience.

8
Considering and Accepting Job Offers

How the Job Offer Is Presented

A verbal offer made by the department head, in person or on the telephone, should be followed by a written offer, stipulating rank, salary, teaching load, and other information. Do not consider yourself officially hired, do not resign your current position, or withdraw yourself from consideration in other searches until you have received and replied to a written offer. You should be given a reasonable amount of time in which to make your decision (in the case of assistant professor usually a week). If the letter states a condition such as "This offer requires the ultimate approval of the President and Trustees," the tender may be withdrawn even after you accept. Act circumspectly. The institution may want to maintain their discretionary powers of veto, particularly because of budgetary considerations, while department chairs and deans want to treat the hiring as settled even if they have acted without final approval. When conditions of hiring have been disputed in court, the decisions handed down have been inconsistent. If possible, stay on the safe side; wait for approval of the offer in writing by the institution's final authority.

Find out if the institution attaches nonacademic rules to faculty positions. There may be codes of deportment that the faculty must observe or creeds they must support or subscribe to, particularly among church-related institutions. You will be told about the latitude of permissible beliefs but perhaps not about other aspects of campus life that you may find you cannot live with.

The formal contract

Some institutions do not use formal contracts, so it is wise to be clear on this point as soon as an offer is made. The letter offering the position and your reply accepting it may constitute the contract where no further document is used. It is important to be satisfied that this letter contains all the specifications that have been made during the final interview. For instance, if this is a tenure-track position, you must have an explicit statement to that effect. If the institution uses formal contracts, presentation of the document for your signature may be delayed until shortly before the academic year. Be sure of the document's contents; the agreement must be made in writing with the corroboration of responsible officials—dean, department head, or whomever has the authoritative word—on what the contract will contain when it is tendered to you.

In the case of public history positions, be sure to find out in advance if restrictions concerning publications or consulting are acceptable to you. Some jobs may require prior clearance of all publications, even if written free-lance. Some agencies have conflict-of-interest rules that may prevent you from engaging in work you want to do on your own time.

Contract negotiations

When an offer is made, in whatever form, it should include precise language on how long the offer will remain in effect—that is, how much time you have to accept it, turn it down, or negotiate revision. Do not be intimidated by the idea of negotiation. It is expected that some negotiation will take place.

Significant revision can be difficult, especially for first-year faculty. You must be extremely alert to all nuances if you intend to negotiate. Your leverage is that the department wants you and wants you to be happy. How far can you push? Do you have a strong case for what you want? Determine these aspects by comparing your situation to similar cases of other new colleagues, if possible, and by how those at the other end of the negotiation table respond to you.

Making the Decision

If you get an offer and you think other schools may be about to approach you, inform the other institutions of the current offer, indicating the time within which you must respond. If other institutions want to compete for your services, they may do so, but do not count on this happening.

Your decision should be based on the realization that the job you choose will play a central role in your life for some time. Evaluate the offer fairly. If you are unsure of any information, contact the department and confirm details. Don't let money cloud the decision-making process. Don't accept one job simply because the starting salary is a few thousand dollars more. Think about future advancement, tenure prospects, living and social environment, and other associated matters. Look at support services, class size, teaching opportunities, sabbatical rules, and benefits packages. Discuss the job offer with family, friends, and colleagues, but trust your own judgment.

After you have accepted a position, it is courteous to write to other institutions that you know have been seriously considering you to tell them of your decision.

Part-time or Short-term Positions

Part-time teaching can mean many things. You could be appointed to a part-time adjunct line, teaching one or more courses, or you could accept a one-to-three-year appointment. These positions will provide you with teaching experience while you are still in graduate school or with employment in the profession while you are applying for more permanent jobs. Some historians also take on adjunct or other part-time teaching to hone their skills while holding other professional positions, such as curatorships.

Grants and funding for limited-duration employment ("soft-money") provide another form of short-term work for historians, allowing many historians to work in the field on special projects for a specified length of time. Some historians have chosen this route to allow for more independence in research and writing.

There are many positive aspects of part-time and short-term work. These options permit involvement in the professional environment without many of the attendant responsibilities of full-time work. It can help to advance long-term goals, especially for beginning historians who cannot yet take on full-time teaching or research jobs because they are still in school. But there are also negative aspects of this type of work. Part-time positions offer schools cheap labor and help them fill situations in an emergency. Most positions lack benefits unless, for example, one is an adjunct for ten years at the same school. This varies, of course, but individuals should carefully weigh these practical considerations with such benefits as mobility and flexibility. If you accept part-time or short-term employment from an institution or through a granting agency, consider checking the faculty or agency guidelines for institutional regulations, as well as state or local policies concerning your rights.

9
Surviving the First Year as a Faculty Member

The most obvious thing about first-year teaching is the staggering amount of time and effort required. You will get up early and stay up late preparing courses, day after day. Even if you think ahead for weeks between landing the job and entering the classroom, the plans will be incomplete and to a surprising extent unsuited to the class. Step back from your graduate student mentality in order to understand what brings undergraduates to the study of history. You should also prepare yourself psychologically to go from the top of the graduate hierarchy to the bottom of the faculty hierarchy. It's a step up but it's a step down, too.

Most colleges publish a faculty handbook that outlines the requirements for hiring faculty members and describes levels of academic and professional competence expected of faculty. You should be given a faculty handbook as soon as you arrive on campus. Read it carefully.

Preparing for Teaching

Many first-year teachers find it helpful to borrow more experienced colleagues' plans for courses as a means of getting started. This will spare you the long labor of contriving courses by yourself the first time through. You might also want to buy teaching packets, such as the Organization of American Historians' "Restoring Women to History: Teaching Packets for Integrating Women's History into Courses on Africa, Asia, Latin America, the Caribbean, and the Middle East." There are a variety of packets of these materials available through the different historical associations. Course syllabi are also now published by different sources, such as Markus Wiener Publishers (see Bibliography, page 103). Send away for lists of such materials as soon as you sign your employment contract and know what you will be teaching.

Responsibilities of a Faculty Member

In addition to preparing your courses, you should also attend to a few other things. Every college or university faculty has committee work, and you must expect to do your share. That means advising and serving on committees for your department and fulfilling other assignments, such as recruiting students or speaking to the public. This is all part of your job. Currently, women and minorities are asked to do more than their share of these tasks in order to diversify the line-up in every academic event. For self-protection, find out what is a normal share of chores and resist taking on too much.

An invaluable survival mechanism for all department faculty who find themselves serving as the women's/African-American/Hispanic/etc. historian is participation in interdisciplinary programs. You may find more peers and more advice in an interdisciplinary program. At the same time, it may also mean that, in effect, you will end up participating in two departments, because such programs often rely heavily on "affiliated faculty" to conduct their business. How will the department reward you if you become affiliated with both the history and an outside department? Discussion about drawbacks and benefits of this dual affiliation would be useful with other department chairs and faculty who are participating in history and interdisciplinary programs. For example, you must find how tenure and promotion will be handled in such situations.

Daily Life in the Department

When you actually arrive in your department office, it is time to learn about the mores and services of office and department culture. You soon will enjoy some departmental services, such as secretarial help, but you may find that a hierarchy exists and, as a beginner, you come last. Learn how to make your requests as easy as possible on the staff and observe the practice of others. You quickly will understand the blessings and limits of clerical support and photocopying. Under no circumstances should you expect the office staff to handle private business. Remember, the staff are professionals and department colleagues.

You may also encounter a formal or informal division of acquisition money for the library. Be sure to use your share.

If you want office furniture or equipment, such as a typewriter, computer, or another chair, put in your request early. Money for such conveniences tends to be scarce, and your department administrator will need a healthy list to make a strong claim for enlarging the department's share. It is best to ask about material things before you accept the job. Deans may have a large budget for initial costs, but once you've started the job without an allocation, it may be too late to request one.

Don't run up the department telephone bill for private calls. Make long-distance calls on professional business only when these are authorized by department regulations.

General Rules-of-Thumb

Learn what counts toward advancement in your position. Formal policies exist but need interpretation. Keep your eyes and ears open to learn what others have done who have succeeded, but don't get too involved in trying to figure out what is appropriate behavior. You should speak when you have something to say, figure out when it's important to fight and when it is wiser to let things go, and work at building credibility as someone who is responsible. Do your departmental homework by reading files for personnel decisions, participating actively in searches, and completing general follow-up tasks, so that you have a chance of winning when it's time to fight.

In addition to an institutional handbook, some departments have a statement that covers most of the ground concerning conditions of employment. Study these guidelines—they will provide you with the foundation for getting along well with your colleagues.

In all likelihood your university's policy is that faculty members must achieve success in the usual trio: teaching, research, and service. That sounds obvious, but learn what is specifically meant by such a policy. At some schools publishing a textbook or other items for classroom use will count in the teaching column, in other schools this applies to research. Some institutions emphasize the number of students in your classes, others look for favorable evaluations by students and faculty. Learn which aspect of teaching is considered important, and what support the school will offer in time, money, computer funds, or other facilities. Find out if the school expects you to bring in research grants.

Service can be an external and vague category. Some schools will accept anything as service—speeches at Rotary Clubs or attendance at professional meetings. Elsewhere, you may find service defined primarily as being for the wider professional community, with everything else given minor attention. Others define service as an exact portion of your time devoted to departmental and collegiate administration. Once you define the categories, you can figure out how to do your best to satisfy the institution's requirements.

Start keeping records and putting documents in your personnel file in the department office. Keep class grade lists, course outlines, notes, and evaluations, if available. Keep copies of anything written for institutional business, publication, or public presentation, as well as reviews of your work. Inform the chair of the department whenever you apply for or get a grant, have something published, or appear on the program of a professional meeting—in fact, anything that contributes to your professional career. Never allow yourself to suffer an incomplete departmental evaluation because of your own negligence. Always fill the gaps in your official file. Conditions for promotions were set before you got the job. Your responsibility is to meet and surpass those conditions. Don't judge your performance by the standards set by some tenured faculty. There is a divergence of expectations, and you'll be asked to accomplish more than the people judging you.

Policies on Family Leave

All employees should be aware of the institution's policies concerning benefits and leaves. Lesbians and gay men, unmarried heterosexual couples, single parents—anyone involved in a domestic partnership, including marriage—should know if the institution's policies include leaves and if certain situations are covered by insurance policies, such as caring for an ill parent, partner, or child, or for maternity or parenting. Make no assumptions about your school's policies. Confirm school/insurance policies in writing with benefits personnel. If the school makes no provision for leaves, you may want to organize to change these policies.

How to Maintain Your Privacy

The new faculty member may face a fairly busy social life. There are ritualistic events, such as a president's reception, a departmental cocktail party, or an all-campus picnic. Ask the chair about protocol whenever you are in doubt. There are still schools where the president's reception is formal. Beyond these obvious rites, you may be invited to parties by your colleagues. You should reciprocate once you are familiar with your colleagues' preferred forms of recreation. Sociability is necessary and enjoyable, in spite of the grueling routine of first-year teaching.

You may find it hard to maintain your privacy during your first year. As the newcomer, you will arouse curiosity. Expect questions from colleagues about your past, your future plans, and your personal life. Some may try to elicit your opinions about the department or school administration. Be careful—first-year stress may be getting to you, and unguarded answers may prove to be a problem later. Do not give in to a negative attitude. Deflect such questions by changing the subject. Handle awkward questions with as much professional aplomb as possible. Your novelty as a newcomer will soon wear off, and by term's end, first-year stresses and demands will abate. Try to weather the storm without giving in to minor grievances. You will make acquaintances and friends worth keeping—even among your most inquisitive colleagues. Try to make the best of the inevitably stressful first year.

Applying for Other Jobs

Once you are employed by an institution, don't feel obliged to stay simply because you feel fortunate to have a job. If you are unhappy with your job, department, or institution, consider a change. With the job market opening up, historians are finding it easier to move laterally within the profession. Consider lateral moves as a serious option at any time in your career. If you do seek another position, make it clear to your department that you are continuing to take seriously your obligations to them. You should place the emphasis on "opportunity" rather than "retreat."

10
Tenure and Promotion

Tenure

In academic life—and in some related professional employments—one of the best-known goals is achieving tenure status. If you do not get tenure, the institution has no obligation to retain your services. If you do, you have security in your job against nearly everything except your own gross dereliction of duty, attrition through change in academic policy, retrenchment, bankruptcy of the school, action of a legislature, or natural disaster.

Tenure is a special relationship between one faculty member and one institution, with benefits to be enjoyed by both parties. The practice of conferring tenure has become so nearly standard throughout American academia as to be regarded as a right by many people. It is no such thing. Most people receive tenure if, and only if, they have satisfied the particular requirements of their institution. To be sure, in some institutions, faculty unions have made conditions for achieving tenure part of a collective rather than individual agreement between employers and employees in a way that seems to make promotion to tenure rather routine.

The requirements for attaining tenure and the procedure for conferring it vary only slightly. Generally, there are time limits. The American Association of University Professors (AAUP) has tried to standardize a probationary period of no more than six years for those hired initially with the PhD and no more than seven years for those hired without it. The decision should be reached during the academic year preceding the last one in the probationary period, so someone passed over may have adequate time to search for another job. Most schools observe something close to this formula but quite a few stretch the probationary period in one way or another, usually in cases of exceptional scholarship and previous teaching experience.

Tenure procedure

Normally the tenure procedure begins with a recommendation from the members of your department who already have tenure. If your department favors your candidacy, their decision goes to the dean, sometimes through a committee composed of faculty from a variety of disciplines—the idea is to achieve some ineffable uniformity of standards or to put a check on the arbitrary will of the dean. If the dean agrees, the recommendation is put before the higher administrators and the institution's governing board, where review is often perfunctory. If the decision at the department level is against you, insist on an explanation, and in that light, perhaps a reconsideration. If the decision is in your favor, the dean may reject it and give reasons. You can appeal an adverse ruling and should learn your institution's procedures for doing so. If you have good reason to fear a negative decision on the basis of gender or racial prejudice, you will want to consult your institution's affirmative action beforehand. (Also see "Dealing with Discrimination" on the next page, and Chapter 12, Grievances, for related information.)

Make sure you are clear about the tenure procedures of your department and college. Seek advice from the relevant staff support in academic personnel or the dean's and president's offices. Your chair may not be aware of all details, and even if you have department backing, the chair may not be able to give you complete information.

Some schools have begun a pretenure evaluation that can be frightening but helpful. In this arrangement, you are looked over in your third or fourth year, or sometimes yearly. Colleagues observe you in the classroom, read your work, and offer a written summary of their thoughts on your progress. This evaluation can let you know how well you are proceeding.

You will be painfully aware of what is going on in your tenure review. Today, in an era of litigiousness and fervor for due process, reviews are more formalized and drawn-out. You will discuss your case with senior colleagues. They may visit your classes, often with elaborate prearrangements that are likely to provoke anxiety. You will take part in preparing your case by going over your record, rounding up copies of your publications, and distributing students' evaluations. You are told the gist of what was said during the actual tenure conference, ostensibly for self-improvement. You may even be in a position to bargain. That is, if you have not met all the requirements, you may be granted a postponement of the final decision.

Dealing with Discrimination

Be prepared to show that others got tenure on the basis of similar records—allowing you to draw comparisons of achievement or to provide well-substantiated allegations of discrimination on the basis of sex, racial, or ethnic background. Regardless of how you frame your case, you will have to gather a great deal of evidence and present it convincingly. Whatever the rules say, the burden of proof is on you, so you may find it helpful to hire a lawyer. You should also ask yourself whether you want to remain with colleagues who have treated you unfairly. Even if you don't, however, the vindication of your professional success may well be worth a fight.

It is far better and far easier to prevent than to undo discrimination against you on nonprofessional grounds. Prejudice against female scholars runs much deeper than it appears, especially if they are feminists, mothers, lesbians, minority women, or commuters. Their writings are often underestimated. As Darlene Clark Hine stated in the summary of the American Studies Association report, "Personal Lives and Professional Careers: The Uneasy Balance":

> Black women professors must tackle head on the problems of having their research and scholarship taken seriously. Women, for the most part, remain recent and still-powerless immigrants in the academy. They still have to work twice as hard and be three times better just to be perceived as average and win tenure and promotion.

No matter what reasons you have for expecting discriminatory treatment in the review for tenure, ask advice from faculty women's/African-American/gay and lesbian/Hispanic or other campus caucuses. Visit the school's affirmative action officer if you think that will help, although sometimes the officer's main concern will be in keeping the university out of lawsuits. The officer can assemble the data to show presumption of a pattern of discrimination or can get the administrators to pay for unusual procedures, such as review of the tenure deliberations by impartial outsiders. Maybe this officer, by monitoring your department, can inspire more scrupulous behavior than would otherwise occur.

If you want to challenge your department's recommendation or the reversal of a favorable recommendation higher up the administrative ladder, consult your local chapter of the AAUP immediately. If there is not a local chapter, contact the AAUP's national headquarters or the American Historical Association.

Promotion

Most institutions rank faculty as assistant, associate, and full professors. Promotion brings a higher salary, more prestige inside and out of the institutions, and often new responsibilities. As an associate or full professor you will be asked to serve on more committees in and out of the institution, and you will be called upon to evaluate for promotion peers in other institutions. Junior faculty will be more likely to regard you as a mentor and to ask for guidance and advice on their professional lives.

If you are a new full-time faculty member with a completed degree, you are usually hired as an assistant professor. You can expect to remain in that position until you are granted tenure and promoted to associate professor. In unusual circumstances, you may be promoted to associate professor before you become eligible for tenure. In most cases, early promotion virtually ensures tenure later on. Sometimes, tenure is awarded without promotion when the faculty member fails to fulfill to the letter the promotion requirements, but the department or institution is willing to grant tenure nonetheless. It bears repeating, however, that such cases are unusual.

Requirements for promotion vary not only at major research universities, but at smaller colleges as well. A record of publication, however, is increasingly an essential element, not only in large universities, but in colleges as well. It is wise to determine your institution's policies as soon as possible. The first few years are difficult; you are busy writing lectures and preparing classes and have little time to pursue research and writing, except in the summer. Beyond the first few years, you should work toward meeting your institution's requirements, and set aside time during the academic year to attend to your own scholarly work.

It is important to attend conferences in your field as well as to publish. It will increase your visibility and help you to develop contacts within your field. Often when you come up for promotion and/or tenure, you are asked to provide a list of individuals who are competent to evaluate your scholarship and overall merit. It is helpful to know about a half dozen people who share your interests and who are sympathetic to your approach. Attending conferences is a good way to get to know people professionally and to keep up with scholarship. It also provides the sort of intellectual exchange that can be difficult to find in institutions where no one shares your particular interests.

Tenure and promotion to associate professor usually occur simultaneously. Although departments generally will specify the time you must spend as an assistant professor before you are promoted, there is no such clear-cut time frame for promotion from associate to full professor. Some people remain associate professors for their entire career; others get promoted within a few years. Usually promotion to full professor requires significant achievement in the years since promotion to the associate level. Time in the ranks alone is rarely sufficient. Here, too, you should try to get a clear sense of what is required to meet the criteria.

Promotion from associate to full professor seems to occur more slowly for women than for men. Some of this is due to sexism, to the unwillingness of colleagues to recognize women's scholarly merit, and to the undervaluation of women's work in the academy as elsewhere. If the woman's scholarly work is in the field of women's history, it may only increase these problems. If you feel you legitimately deserve promotion and are being denied it on sexist grounds, do something about it. In some cases, women's careers simply proceed more slowly. As a mother, you might want to spend more time with your children after receiving tenure and promotion. You will certainly find that you have more demands on your time, all of which make it difficult to find the time to publish, which is generally a requirement for promotion to full professor. In most academic institutions, women associate professors are still a minority. Women are nevertheless called upon to participate as faculty members on committees that strive for gender balance, to advise women students, to mentor junior faculty women, and to fulfill a variety of other roles. Since tenured women are a scarce commodity, and there are still too few to go around, it is very easy for a woman associate (or full) professor to become overcommitted and to neglect teaching and research, which are supposed to be the primary focuses. This requires hard choices. If you want to be promoted but feel a sense of responsibility to the women in your institution, you will have to work a lot harder than most of your male peers. It helps to learn to say no and to weigh choices and commitments carefully.

11
The Professional Couple

The academic job market has changed dramatically in the past two decades. Increasingly, professionals are in partner/spousal relationships with other professionals. No longer is it possible for an employer to hire an individual (typically male) and assume that this individual's dependents will unhesitatingly accept the collective implications of an individual career decision. This trend shows absolutely no signs of abating; indeed, in coming years, it will most probably accelerate. Unfortunately, few employers have found adequate solutions to this dramatic change in the labor market. Many continue to base their expectations on patterns that no longer exist.

Commuter Relationships—and Stress

Balancing the needs of personal relationships against the priorities of finding work in your profession can be excruciatingly difficult. Solutions that leave everyone happy are rare. A commuting relationship adds stress to an already stressful life, and a salary can disappear into plane fares, phone bills, and the expense of a second residence. Participation in a conference becomes not just time away from course preparation, the book review that's overdue, and the chance to read the Sunday paper, but also time away from your partner. This can be difficult for couples with a relatively easy commute, but it is even harder for couples who have to live apart.

The rigors of commuting will cut into the time you would otherwise have to make a home in the community in which you work, to find new friends, and to catch your breath. For commuting couples with children, all these problems are immediately magnified. Colleagues—particularly older men, who are married to women without careers or jobs that conflict with their husband's goals—may have little understanding of your situation and may view you with suspicion. They will have even less sympathy for the same problems that confront nonmarried couples, whether heterosexual, gay, or lesbian. Indeed, in these cases, you will have to consider how open you can be about your personal relationships.

These problems obviously exist when both partners are academics, but they are of no less significance for a historian in a relationship with a pediatrician, social worker, schoolteacher, lawyer, or any other professional. The belief that some professionals are more mobile and readily employable than others becomes quite problematic when an East Coast urban lawyer who thrives on litigation must relocate to the rural Midwest. Not only must a lawyer pass the new state's bar in most cases, but legal networks are often of a local nature. Similarly, a schoolteacher with accreditation in one state often finds that the certification is not easily transferred to another without further course work. Career moves can also mean leaving behind friends, relationships, and survival networks, which can be as important to your partner as the satisfaction of a particular job.

Living Apart

The myth that long separations enhance the quality of a relationship is typically most popular among those who aren't in such a relationship themselves.

Anyone who is involved in a commuting relationship will be able to come up with their own anxiety-producing list. However, they will also be just as able to offer good reasons for taking on such hardships; the drawbacks of living apart from your partner or commuting always have to be weighed against the alternative of one partner giving up a career or "retooling" in order for the other to pursue a chosen field. The costs of this decision can be immense, and for most professional couples, they far outweigh the costs of dealing with an indefinite period of living apart.

Taking Advantage of Leave Policies

While you are searching for employment possibilities closer together, there are a number of strategies you can pursue. Having an academic job means that you can take leaves. If you know you and your partner will have to live apart, it becomes even more important to establish your department's policy on leaves and time off for extramural grants *before* you accept a position. You will have to weigh the advantages and disadvantages of letting your employer know your personal circumstances, but at the very least, you can determine what possibilities exist for time off.

Take advantage of the enormous flexibility of academic schedules. No other job gives you as much as twenty to twenty-five weeks a year when your employer need not know where you are working. No other job gives you such lengthy uninterrupted periods when you can leave your place of employment.

In addition, as employers become more and more concerned about retirement waves and the increasing difficulties of recruitment, there are at least some signs that an individual faced with the prospect of a commuting relationship can make specific inquiries into ways to ease the situation. Because the institution wants to hire you, your colleagues may be willing to make certain accommodations, such as adjusting the demands of your teaching schedule to your commuting schedule or allowing you to teach fewer courses. Knowing when to ask about such possibilities can be tricky. You'll have to rely on your judgment and the advice of others who confront similar circumstances at your campus or in your department. If you find that your department is totally unsympathetic to your dilemma, then you should continue to study the EIB, in the American Historical Association's monthly *Perspectives;* other employers may be more flexible and sympathetic.

Job Sharing

Splitting an academic position is another possibility. If you determine that you can survive on one salary and your partner is also a historian, you can consider this alternative. There are at least some indications that history departments are beginning to realize that such a solution is definitely to their advantage. If the school is receptive to this, you should verify policies regarding promotion and salary reviews, sabbatical leaves, and other benefits.

The AHA's Committee on Women Historians is currently considering possible recommendations on partner/spousal policies for the profession.

12
Grievances

Most colleges and universities have developed quasi-judicial procedures for hearing grievances. Under the best circumstances, procedures are written and all members of faculty and staff receive copies of the rules. In other cases, less is committed to paper and the institution does little to make the procedures known. If this is the case at your institution, you might want to consider organizing to formalize grievance procedures. All levels of faculty and students deserve legitimate and fair recourse for grievances.

In all probability, most grievances will be internal and will raise questions that belong in the department. Many complaints can be addressed in a conference with your department chair or supervisor. The supervisor's job is to facilitate the faculty's professional endeavors. A conscientious chair should take your word for what will benefit the department and will look for ways to settle any conflicts.

Conflicts may occur between you and your supervisor, however, and usually a short discussion with the person next up the ladder, such as a dean, will suffice. Maybe you will think better of the case and withdraw the complaint. Maybe your dean will speak to your immediate supervisor. When going through these channels, resist any urges you have to talk generally on your feelings about the institution. Stick to the immediate issues, and always state your problem in professional terms. Any indication of personal gripes is likely to be received with impatience or dismissed.

Faculty committees may be part of the grievance procedure. They may evaluate applications for research grants or special awards for launching new courses, advise the dean on promotions or tenure, guard against rejecting deserved promotions and raises. If you think you have been wronged by one of these committees, it may be difficult to bring a complaint. The committees are intended to make decisions on the basis of collective evaluations rather than individual judgments, so the members are obliged to say little about their deliberations. Your best bet is to consult the relevant dean or to discreetly ask friends who know members of the committee. You must know precisely what your complaint is about and how to express it and prove it, if you are to make a successful claim. If these methods fail, look around to find a plausible next step for your appeal. You may also have to consider the possibility that your hopes have been unreasonable.

The most likely trouble spot is an abusive administration where the grievance procedures are likely to be absent or rudimentary. If grievance procedures exist, the administrators may try to keep them out of sight. In other cases, department chairs have been known to deny a faculty member's request for access to the university's operations manual or budget. In the face of such conduct, you may feel helpless. Help may be available from the dean or may require outside consultation. Your first task is to find a way to initiate action to protect yourself. First ask your chair, then the dean or other colleagues, about applicable rules—where you can read them and which appeals are open to you. It is important to verify procedures in writing whenever possible.

If your institution offers a quasi-judicial grievance hearing, use it when the situation requires it. Speak to the school's affirmative action officer or, if necessary, consider consulting a lawyer. There is a growing body of law and precedent on these hearings, which a good attorney will be able to explain.

Where local channels are blocked or do not exist, write to the American Association of University Professors' national headquarters and to the American Historical Association. The AAUP will look into your complaint and will make a concerted effort to determine and redress wrongs without embarrassing the complainant (plaintiff). The AHA's Professional Division looks into grievances brought to its attention but follows strict policy rules pertaining to such procedures. The AHA also generally has a policy of staying out of such disputes until procedures on the complainant's local level have been pursued to little or no avail.

13
How to Get on a Program at a Professional Meeting

The Role of the Program Committee

Program committees are required to develop a program that is balanced geographically, chronologically, and topically. To do so, they generally welcome proposals from a variety of potential participants. Some program committees prefer to select commentators themselves; others gladly take suggestions. The following will hardly guarantee your participation but should increase your chances by describing some of the elements a program committee will look for.

Getting onto a Program

Subject

In order to make your proposal as strong as possible, try to submit a complete panel rather than a single paper, although the latter is acceptable. Individual papers should clearly relate and should focus on historically significant problems.

Participants

In choosing participants, your first aim should be a strong panel. You should make every effort to find historians who have not been program participants in the past year. Balance the panel with regard to gender, minorities, rank, regions, and type of institution. If papers are to be given by younger members of the profession, it is often desirable that at least one of the commentators be a person of established reputation.

Submitting the panel

Have one person coordinate all of the papers and write up the proposal so that a unified panel is submitted. Briefly explain in the cover letter the purpose and significance of the panel and its appropriate historical categories. For example, one panel might be American history, family history, and urban history. Include relevant background information on participants. Explain their expertise in the subjects under discussion. Be concise and to the point.

Enclose a description of the panel as it would appear in the program. This includes titles for the session and the papers. Consult an old program for form and study the guidelines in calls for papers. Provide a brief statement about the panel's purpose and importance with a short summary of each paper's thesis or program. Keep the entire statement short and succinct.

Submit the proposal early

Submit the proposal well in advance of the deadlines. Send the proposal and cover letter to the program committee chair. The chair keeps a log of all plans submitted and sends copies for appraisal to the members of the committee who are particularly concerned with each field. The member who reviews your proposal may write to you about it, asking you to clarify questions. It is your responsibility to check journals, newsletters, and so forth, for information on deadlines as well as program committee membership. Some programs are prepared almost two years in advance, so don't allow the time to slip by you.

If the proposal is turned down and you are convinced it is a sound plan, consider offering it again the following year. Your topics may have been unusually popular at that meeting. In any event, be prepared to wait several months after the committee's deadline for final notification of acceptance or rejection. In the meantime, however, you may receive word of tentative approval from the chair or an encouraging hint from the member who evaluated your proposal.

Presenting the paper

Once you have agreed to participate in a session, make every effort to fulfill that agreement. If you are to read a paper, allow ample time to write the very best one you can. In most cases, you will be told exactly how long your presentation should be, so plan accordingly. You can count on reading a page in about two minutes, so keep your paper short enough to stay within the time assigned. The person who chairs the session has the duty to cut off presentations after the allotted time has expired. You don't want to be asked to sit down just before you have reached that eloquent climax. Also, make sure you submit a copy of your paper to the panel's commentators, normally one month ahead of time.

As you prepare your paper, remember that several people, perhaps prospective employers, may request a copy. While the organization and style of the text will be designed for a listening audience, use the footnotes to gear your paper to your reading audience as well.

Always give your paper an advance performance, if possible before a large audience. Women might think of a women's caucus within their department, but if your department has a colloquium that draws a larger crowd and you feel comfortable with the paper and the audience, take advantage of this opportunity to rehearse. Junior faculty may find that this experience can become an ersatz midcareer review, a second job talk, or a pretenure review, and choose not to engage in this anxiety-producing effort. Nevertheless, the best criticism often comes from colleagues whose fields and perspectives differ from your own.

One of the major goals in presenting a paper may be to build your c.v. But remember that the more important goal is to share your ideas and receive responses to them from the audience. Go into your session prepared for this intellectual give-and-take.

14
Getting Published

Historians communicate scholarship orally, visually, and in writing. They teach and speak; create and consult on media projects, exhibits, or other cultural resources; and they publish. For scholars, publishing is an important way to communicate the result of scholarship. Publishing is one of the responsibilities as well as one of the joys of being a historian, and most historians enjoy both research and writing.

As a historian, you will want to present your scholarship in various ways to the broadest possible audience, but you will also want to communicate to colleagues in a more specialized language. Learn how to present your work in different styles for different audiences, but make sure that it is always based on careful research, written in excellent prose, and has a broad intellectual scope. Never publish anything but the best work you are capable of.

Academic historians are expected by colleagues and school administrations to document their scholarly activities in a particular way during their initial untenured years. It is best to learn as much as possible about the process in graduate school, from peers and publishers. Promotion often rests with the perception of your publication record, so you must be conscious of how your colleagues judge publishing. If you know what criteria they use, you will be able to present your work in the most effective way. Public historians must balance the requirements of their varied activities and publication in public history against writing and research that focus more narrowly on traditional history.

How much publishing is enough? Standards vary by department. Seek out and familiarize yourself with departmental guidelines regarding publication for promotion and tenure. These policies should be clearly stated by your employer and must guide your publication strategy.

Finding a Publisher for a Monograph or Book

Normally, the scholarly monograph is viewed by the profession as the most significant work to publish for promotion and tenure.

Some departments will be content just to see your manuscript; others will insist on seeing a contract or even a published book.

These differing demands may dictate your publishing strategy. Never publish a book that you do not consider an important contribution to the literature of your field, but do not expect your first book to be a "great book." Make it as good as you can, send it into the world, and look forward to your next effort. Be aware that different publishers have different timetables and different reputations for efficiency and treatment of authors. Do not be afraid to call several scholars who have published with a press to find out how they were treated.

You may send a query and a proposal to more than one editor, but once a press asks to read your manuscript, do not submit it to anyone else for consideration until you know whether or not that publisher wants to publish your work. A proposal should contain the following:

1. Submit a brief description of the scope of the book, the sources used, methodologies employed, and its significance to the literature in the field.

2. Suggest a potential market. Would it be useful in courses in paperback? Who would read it and why?

3. Indicate the length of the manuscript, sections that are incomplete, need revision, or require scholarly updates. If the manuscript is or was a dissertation, state your plans for revision, as a dissertation *will* need editing and revision before it can be published as a book.

4. Include information on the form of the manuscript. If your book has been written on a word processor, indicate the kind of software used. Some publishers may not use authors' diskettes, so keep the format and files simple. Do not use elaborate codes to indicate chapter, sub-, or chart heads with bold or italic type or symbols, since these will be reformatted to fit the publisher's design and typesetting equipment. If the publisher requests a copy of the manuscript, submit two clean, easy-to-read copies. Charts or illustrations may be submitted on separate sheets. Any marks on the manuscript should be made clearly and in pencil.

5. Enclose a copy of your c.v.

Your cover letter may mention persons in the field who are competent to judge the manuscript. The editor, however, is not obliged to follow your suggestions. It is wise to exclude friends and mentors to avoid the possibility of favoritism or bias.

To find a publisher for your work, study ads, publishers' lists, and the *Literary Market Place* or the *Writer's Market*. Other good sources of information are the updated edition of the American Historical Association's *A Guide to Book Publication for Historians,* and *Getting Published: The Acquisition Process at University Presses,* published by University of Tennessee Press. (See Bibliography, page 103.)

Editors will usually read your manuscript, pay an honorarium to outside readers for an evaluation, and prepare reports for their publications board on the commercial viability of publishing your work. Time and money is invested in the decision to publish and once a publisher has expressed an interest in your work, *it is not appropriate to negotiate with two publishers over the same manuscript.* Evaluate potential publishers and send the manuscript to your first choice, then to succeeding ones who have expressed interest, indicating that other publishers are also reading your manuscript. If your manuscript is ultimately rejected by a publisher who was seriously considering it, you are then free to submit it to another press. If the publisher suggests revisions that you are not prepared to make, you may cut off negotiations and begin the process with another publisher.

Once you have been notified of an editor's interest in your manuscript, you will doubtless have questions about the publishing process. Many questions cannot be addressed until the manuscript is accepted and a contract offered, but here are some questions to keep in mind when entering into serious discussions with the publisher:

- How long to find out if the manuscript is accepted for publication?
- How long for contract negotiations?
- How long will production take?
- What are the publisher's plans for marketing?
- How many copies will be printed?
- Will hardcover and paperback editions be published?
- Will the paperback be published simultaneously?
- If not, how long before the paperback is released?
- What are, if any, the royalty agreements/advances?

If you have any doubts about the answers you receive, be sure to speak to other authors to get a different perspective. Do not act hastily. Consider all factors: editing, marketing, rights and royalties, contract negotiations, and a publisher's reputation before deciding on one publisher over another.

Dealing with Rejections

All authors accumulate rejection letters. You will, too. If the scholarship and interpretations you present are sound, you will eventually find a publisher. Determine if the rejection was due to general publishing decision-making or the product. Sometimes budgetary or other considerations may be the cause of the rejection. If you are unsure about your writing style, study historians whose style you admire. Or sign up for a technical writing workshop at your university. These courses are often very helpful for learning good expository writing techniques and for developing organizing strategies. Ask colleagues, other scholars, or mentors to review the work.

A rejection may simply mean that you have not found the right publisher. Seek advice from colleagues whose work your respect. Continue to look for editors who are likely to be interested in your subject. Query letters may bring ten to twenty rejections for every one or two invitations to read the manuscript. Normally you will want to try two or three presses before beginning major revisions or resubmission. If the problem seems to be scholarship, interpretation, or style—or all three—you must be prepared to reevaluate and revise your manuscript, based on the demands of your job and private life, as well as those of the press.

Publication Procedures

It will take about a year from the time you submit the manuscript until you see a finished book. Usually the copy editor's revisions and final page proofs can be managed along with your other professional responsibilities, but once the contract is signed and the book goes into production, your job may be far from over. Depending on the publisher's schedule and budget, you may be asked to approve editing; proofread and correct the typeset pages; compile the index; provide clean, easily reproduced charts, tables, maps, or illustrations—all in a relatively short period of time. Personal and professional demands may compete with publication deadlines. Whenever possible, it would be to your advantage to try to schedule large projects, such as indexing, during school breaks. This is not always possible based on publishing schedules, but it is worth inquiring about. A possible alternative would be to hire an indexer. However, this often costs several hundred dollars, and you may be required to pay for such free-lance services. There are indexing software packages available, and this may be a good solution. Such concerns should be addressed during contract negotiations.

Problems within a Publishing House

Stability is important in any business relationship, particularly when dealing with a publisher and editor. If a publisher sells out or merges, you may be faced with a suspended publishing program. A publisher may try to cancel or buy out your contract or publish but not market your book. Transitions at small or large commercial publishers can be difficult to weather. University presses tend to be more stable, but editors still move around. Practices vary depending on where you are. Adjustment to changes in staff at your publisher can also be trying and problematic. Your editor may move to another press and want to take you along, if you have not already signed a contract. A new editor may be in a different field or have different interests and not recognize your contribution as quickly as another.

Publishing Articles in Scholarly Journals

Make sure you know which journals the profession as a whole and your colleagues in particular consider the most scholarly and prestigious. If you are in a field about which your colleagues know little, you should explain in a memo to the department why this journal is important in the field. If you publish in journals not well-known to historians, try to achieve a balance by submitting articles to journals that are better known in the profession. Should you be unable to do so, there may be consequences in terms of recognition and evaluation of your work by colleagues and administration. While it is important to reach the widest possible audience with your writing, in the early years of your career it is necessary to balance this goal carefully against the reality that the department and university within which you are seeking tenure will almost always be the final arbiter.

Articles relating to your book

Resist the tendency to cannibalize your book by publishing chapters. If possible, maintain the integrity of your work by publishing it whole, while the material is fresh, so you do not jeopardize your chance to reach the best possible audience. Publishing one article is a good idea because it establishes you as an authority on the subject, alerts others in your field to your larger work, brings criticism from scholars that you can incorporate into the final version of your book, and may attract the attention of a potential editor. Many journals have backlogs, so remember that publication of an article may take longer than publication of the book. Also be aware that book publishers often prefer to be the first to publish your work, so before submitting an article or chapter from your book to a journal, it may be wise to negotiate this first with your publisher.

If you have research that was collected during your project but will not be included in the book, by all means submit it separately to a journal. In the explanatory note indicate how it relates to your larger work. If an article is based on your dissertation, list the dissertation title in a footnote. However, do not mention a title for an as-yet-unpublished book. Titles often change in the publishing process, and if you publish an incorrect title, it will haunt you for years as your future colleagues or students attempt to locate your book and cannot find it.

Book Reviews

Writing book reviews is a part of your life as a scholar. To receive book review work, register with the *Journal of American History* and the *American Historical Review* and specialized journals such as the *Journal of the Early Republic, Social Science History,* or *Journal of Women's History.* Most journals have forms that you are asked to fill out to let the editor know your special fields of expertise. You may also ask to review an individual book if you have special knowledge in the field or something important to say about a particular work. Do not ask or consent to review books written by friends or mentors. Professional acquaintance, however, is no reason to reject an invitation to review a book unless you feel somehow unable to provide a careful, objective analysis of the book, or you feel somehow that if you reviewed an acquaintance's book, it would unduly promote or sabotage the work.

Given your time constraints, do not review too many books. You might consider applying the "rule of two." Two a year is plenty unless you are asked to review an important book for an important journal. How do you decide which review work to accept and which to refuse? As mentioned earlier, ask colleagues which journals they read and respect. This has the added advantage of knowing how they will consider your reviews. If opinions differ widely about which journals to submit book reviews to, seek opinions from a broader range of your colleagues, and try to get a consensus.

Finding the time to write and sign on with a publisher for your monographs is a challenge to any beginning historian. As you progress in the profession, you may find that your schedule will permit more time to devote to publishing. There is a great deal of information on publishing available if you know where to look. Make a point of keeping up with publishers' catalogs and the book review sections of major journals, even if you only have time to skim through them.

Conclusion

Becoming a Historian: A Survival Manual for Women and Men has given the novice historian a necessarily brief glimpse into a vast and varied field. This overview was intended to advise and interest students in a profession that by definition continually redefines itself. Concerns about better opportunities for women, people of color, and gays and lesbians have yet to be specifically addressed in many areas of the profession. A chief aim of this manual has been to promote the many benefits and positive aspects of the historical profession: the reward of service, the scholarly achievement, and the intellectual stimulation of steady growth and learning. Another necessary aim, however, has been to alert, inform, and empower students when faced with some of the inequities within the profession.

The historical profession can offer women and men a variety of careers and chances to broaden and refine intellectual interests. Although academia is the largest area of employment, positions in public history, archives, and other specialized fields have grown in recent years. It is the author's and contributors' hope that *Becoming a Historian: A Survival Manual for Women and Men* offers ideas to beginning historians, and the incentive to take advantage of—and eventually contribute to—the wealth of resources available. The "how-tos" of choosing a field of study, writing effective applications, finding funding, dealing with the tension of job searches, interviewing, and survival upon first entering the profession have hopefully provided you with practical, applicable advice. Forethought, skill, and diligence will accomplish the rest.

APPENDIX A: A CHECKLIST OF JOB INTERVIEW QUERIES

The following is a checklist of questions and concerns to bear in mind as you interview. The information is addressed to historians in an academic environment, but the details pertain to public historians' concerns as well. When considering a major professional or geographic move, this information may help you to make an often difficult decision.

ACADEMIC CONCERNS

Teaching and Pedagogy
- subjects
- undergraduate/graduate courses
- class size/average academic ability of students
- course development opportunities
- examination policies
- textbook policies: required/optional
- teaching/research assistants
- equipment resources: audiovisual media, maps
- student/graduate thesis advising
- committee membership responsibilities

ADMINISTRATIVE CONCERNS

Office
- size/location
- equipment: typewriter/computer; bookshelves, filing cabinets, phone

Department/Institutional Support Services
- secretarial/clerical help
- manuscript preparation
- wordprocessing capabilities
- computer services
- statistical/data analysis software availability
- photocopying services
- graphics/printing capabilities
- telephone/fax/telecommunications/mail facilities/policies

Governance Systems
- •department/faculty/institutional/campus
- •local/county/city/state legislative

Campus Security
- •parking/other transportation
- •security personnel
- •distribution of keys/passes
- •grounds lighting
- •campus emergency services:
  phones/fire/police/medical facilities

Resources
- •library facilities: monograph/serial
  holdings; reserve policies; audiovisual
  materials/microfilm/microfiche; purchasing
  policies/interlibrary loan services; support
  staff; faculty carrels

BENEFITS

- •Promotion/tenure policies
- •Salary: review/raise policies
- •Retirement policies: TIAA/CREF or other programs
- •Credit union within institution
- •Health insurance: dental, optical, full medical
- •Maternity leave
- •Child care provision
- •Travel/leave policy

RESEARCH AND PROFESSIONAL DEVELOPMENT

Faculty Teaching Development and Support
- •departmental/college faculty seminars
- •local funding programs
- •support for regional/national grant proposals
- •campus grants officer

Research Support
- •conferences/research: grants or
  leaves/seminars/workshops

COMMUNITY ENVIRONMENT

Cost of Living
- housing: availability
- Local/state tax structure
- insurance: home/car
- food/services/entertainment

Community Resources
- public safety services: fire/police/ambulance
  snow emergency services/road maintenance
- parking and public transportation
- recycling programs
- community groups
- car repair
- shopping/banking
- local medical services
- daycare facilities/public and private schools
- libraries
- religious services

Entertainment and Recreation
- indoor/outdoor activities
- restaurants
- community clubs/organiztions
- theaters: movie/local stage company
- sports
- nightlife
- arts community

Local Government
- local/county/city/state/legislative

APPENDIX B: SELECTED PROFESSIONAL ORGANIZATIONS

Listed below are a handful of organizations that graduate students and novice historians will find relevant to their pursuit for information about the historical profession. Much of the text is derived from *Careers for Students of History*, by Barbara J. Howe, and published by the American Historical Association and the National Council on Public History. This is by no means a complete list nor is it a recommendation. The *Directory of Affiliated Societies*, which is published annually by the AHA, is also a good resource. The *Directory of Federal Historical Programs and Activities*, published triennially by the Society for History in the Federal Government, the AHA, and the National Coordinating Committee for the Promotion of History, should be helpful to those interested in public history programs. The most recent edition was published in 1990. Finally, the annual *Encyclopedia of Associations* provides information on thousands of organizations. It should be available, along with other comprehensive resources, at major public and school libraries.

ACT Student Need Analysis Service, P.O. Box 1002, Iowa City, Iowa 52243

Advisory Council on Historic Preservation, 1100 Pennsylvania Ave. NW, Washington, D.C. 20004 (202-254-3967)

Affirmative Action Inc., 8356 Olive Blvd., St. Louis, Mo. 63132

American Association for State and Local History, 172 Second Ave. North, Suite 102, Nashville, Tenn. 37201 (615-255-2971)

American Association of Community and Junior Colleges, National Center for Higher Education, One Dupont Circle NW, No. 410, Washington, D.C. 20036 (202-293-7050)

American Association of Museums, 1225 Eye St. NW, Suite 200, Washington, D.C. 20005 (202-289-1818)

American Association of University Professors, 1012 14th St. NW, Suite 500, Washington, D.C. 20005 (202-737-5900)

American Bar Association, 750 N. Lake Shore Dr., Chicago, Ill. 60611 (312-988-5000)

American College Testing Program, P.O. Box 168, Iowa City, Iowa 52243

American Historical Association, 400 A St. SE, Washington, D.C. 20003 (202-544-2422)

American Library Association, 50 E. Huron St., Chicago, Ill. 60611 (312-944-6780)

American Studies Association, 2100 Taliaferro Bldg., University of Maryland, College Park, Md. 20742 (301-454-2533)

Association for Documentary Editing, c/o Elizabeth Hughes, Papers of Dwight D. Eisenhower, Department of History, Johns Hopkins University, Baltimore, Md. 21218 (301-338-8363)

Association for Living Historical Farms and Agricultural Museums, Smithsonian Institution, National Museum of American History, Room 5035, Washington, D.C. 20560 (202-357-2095)

Association of American Publishers, 2005 Massachusetts Ave. NW, Washington, D.C. 20036 (202-232-3335)

Association of American University Presses, One Park Ave., New York, N.Y. 10016 (212-889-6040)

Association of Black Women Historians, Janice Sumler-Lewis, National Director, 716 Ridgecreek Dr., Clarkston, Ga. 30021

Berkshire Conference of Women Historians, Barbara J. Harris, Women's Studies Program, University of North Carolina, Chapel Hill, N.C. 27599-3135

College Placement Council, 62 Highland Ave., Bethlehem, Pa. 18017 (215-868-1421)

College Scholarship Service (CSS). *See listing for Educational Testing Service.*

Committee on Lesbian and Gay History, John C. Fout, Coordinator, Department of History, Bard College, Annandale-on-Hudson, N.Y. 12504

Community College Humanities Association, 1700 Spring Garden St., Philadelphia, Pa. 19130 (215-751-0002)

Conference of Historical Journals, Department of History, Appalachian State University, Boone, N.C. 28608 (704-262-2282)

Coordinating Committee on Women in the Historical Profession, Lynn Weiner, Executive Director, 527 S. Clinton, Oak Park, Ill. 60304

Editorial Freelancers Association, P.O. Box 2050, Madison Square Station, New York, N.Y. 10159 (212-677-3357)

Educational Career Service, P.O. Box 672, Princeton, N.J. 08540-0672

Educational Testing Service (ETS), Rosedale Road, Princeton, N.J. 08541 (609) 921-9000

Federation of State Humanities Councils, 1012 14th St. NW, Suite 1007, Washington, D.C. 20005 (202-393-5400)

Historians Film Committee, c/o History Faculty, New Jersey Institute of Technology, Newark, N.J. 07102 (201-596-3269)

Institute of Museum Services, 1100 Pennsylvania Ave. NW, Room 510, Washington, D.C. 20506 (202-786-0539)

National Archives and Records Administration, 8th St. and Pennsylvania Ave. NW, Washington, D.C. 20408 (202-523-3218)

National Center for the Study of History, Inc., c/o RR 1, Box 679, Cornish, Maine 04020 (301-770-1174)

National Coalition of Independent Scholars, 105 Vicente Road, Berkeley, Calif. 94705

National Conference of State Historic Preservation Officers, Hall of the States, Suite 332, 444 North Capitol St. NW, Washington, D.C. 20001 (202-624-5465)

National Coordinating Committee for the Promotion of History, 400 A St. SE, Washington, D.C. 20003 (202-544-2422)

National Council for Preservation Education, Department of History, Georgia State University, Atlanta, Ga. 30303 (404-658-3255)

National Council for the Social Studies, 3501 Newark St. NW, Washington, D.C. 20016 (202-966-7840)

National Council on Public History, 403 Richards Hall, Northeastern University, Boston, Mass. 02115 (617-437-2677)

National Endowment for the Arts, 1100 Pennsylvania Ave. NW, Washington, D.C. 20506 (202-682-5400)

National Endowment for the Humanities, 1100 Pennsylvania Ave. NW, Washington, D.C. 20506 (202-786-0438)

National Historical Publications and Records Commission, National Archives and Records Administration, 8th St. and Pennsylvania Ave. NW, Washington, D.C. 20408 (202-523-1701)

National Register of Historic Places, National Park Service, P.O. Box 37127, U.S. Department of the Interior, Washington, D.C. 20013-7127 (202-343-9536)

National Society for Internships and Experiential Education, 122 St. Mary's St., Raleigh, N.C. 27605 (919-787-3263)

National Trust for Historic Preservation, 1785 Massachusetts Ave. NW, Washington, D.C. 20036 (202-673-4000)

The Newspaper Guild, 8611 Second Ave., Silver Spring, Md. 20910

Oral History Association, Executive Secretariat, 1093 Broxton Avenue, #720, Los Angeles, Calif. 90024 (213-825-7524)

Organization of American Historians, 112 N. Bryan St., Bloomington, Ind. 47401 (812-335-7311)

Organization of History Teachers, c/o Earl P. Bell, President, University High School, 1362 East 59th St., Chicago, Ill. 60637 (312-702-0588)

Phi Alpha Theta, 2333 Liberty St., Allentown, Pa. 18104 (215-433-4140)

Popular Culture Association, Department of Popular Culture, Bowling Green State University, Bowling Green, Ohio 43402 (419-372-7865)

Society for Historians of the Early American Republic, Department of History, Lebanon Valley College, Annville, Pa. 17003 (717-867-6100)

Society for History Education, Inc., California State University, Long Beach, Calif. 90840 (213-985-4503)

Society for History in the Federal Government, Box 14139, Ben Franklin Station, Washington, D.C. 20044

Society for Scholarly Publishing, West 44th Avenue, Wheatridge, Colorado 80033 (303-422-3914)

Society of American Archivists, 600 S. Federal St., Suite 504, Chicago, Ill. 60605 (312-922-0140)

U.S. Government, Office of Personnel Management, 1900 E St. NW, Washington, D.C. 20415 (202-653-8468)

Western History Association, Department of History, University of Nevada, Reno, Nev. 89557 (702-784-6852)

Women in Scholarly Publishing, Indiana University Press, 10th and Morton Sts., Bloomington, Ind. 47405 (812-335-5429)

Women's National Book Association, 160 Fifth Ave., New York, N.Y. 10010 (212-675-7804)

APPENDIX C: SELECTED BIBLIOGRAPHY

This is a selected bibliography of publications by the professional organizations which are affiliated with the historical profession. It is not intended as a comprehensive list or a recommendation of these organizations' publications. If no publication information is given, the publication cited is a periodical. Most addresses not listed here can be found in Appendix B.

Affirmative Action Register, 8356 Olive Blvd., St. Louis, Missouri 63132.

American Association for State and Local History. *History News; History News Dispatch; Directory of Historical Societies and Agencies; Directory of Historical Organizations in the United States and Canada,* 14th ed, Mary Bray Wheeler, ed. *The Wages of History: The AASLH Employment Trends and Salary Survey,* by Charles Phillips and Patricia Hogan; *On Doing Local History: Reflections on What Local Historians Do, Why, and What it Means,* by Carol Kammen; and an extensive list of books, audiovisual materials, and technical leaflets.

American Association of Community and Junior Colleges. *AACJC Letter, Community Technical and Junior College Journal,* and *Community Technical and Junior College Directory.*

American Association of Museums. *Museums News; Aviso;* "Careers in Museums: A Variety of Vocations, Resource Report 2"; *The 1988 Official Museum Directory.* Wilmette, Ill.: National Register Publishing Co., 1988.

American Association of University Professors. *Academe* and *Collective Bargaining Newsletter.*

American Historical Association. *American Historical Review; Perspectives; Directory of History Departments and Organizations in the United States and Canada; Directory of Federal Historical Programs and Activities* (with the Society for History in the Federal Government and the National Coordinating Committee for the Promotion of History); *Directory of Women Historians; Doctoral Dissertations in History; Grants, Fellowships, & Prizes of Interest to Historians; A Guide to Book Publication for Historians,* rev. ed., by Norman Fiering; *Careers for Students of History,* by Barbara J. Howe (with the National Council on Public History); "Liberal Learning and the History Major" (in cooperation with the American Association of Colleges; "Statement on Standards of Professional Conduct"; and *Preparation of Secondary-School History Teachers,* 3rd ed., rev., by Donald B.Cole and Thomas Pressly.

Association for Documentary Editing. *Documentary Editing.*

Association of American Publishers. *AAP Monthly Report and Newsletter.*

Association of American University Presses. *Exchange.*

Barron's Profiles of American Colleges. Hauppauge, N.Y.: Barron's Educaitonal Series.

Baxter, Neale. *Opportunities in Federal Government Careers* and *Opportunities in State and Local Government Careers.* Lincolnwood, Ill.: National Textbook Co., 1985.

Belisle, May. *Humanists on the Move: Employment Patterns for Humanities Ph.D.s.* Washington, D.C.: National Academy Press, 1985.

Benson, Susan Porter; Stephen Brier; and Roy Rosenzweig, eds. *Presenting the Past: Essays on History and the Public.* Philadelphia: Temple University Press, 1986.

Bettor, Dorothy K. *Aside From Teaching, What in the World Can You Do? Career Strategies for Liberal Arts Graduates.* Seattle: University of Washington, 1982.

Bolles, Richard N. *What Color Is Your Parachute?* 1990 revised edition, Ten Speed Press, P.O. Box 7123, Berkeley, California 94707.

Bradley Commission on History in Schools. *Building a History Curriculum: Guidelines for Teaching History in Schools.* Washington, D.C.: Educational Excellence Network, 1988.

Burcaw, G. Ellis. *Introduction to Museum Work.* Nashville, Tenn.: American Association for State and Local History, 1983.

Butterworth, Amy. *The National Directory of Internships.* Raleigh, N.C.: National Society for Internships and Experiential Education, 1989.

Career Associates. *Career Choices for Students of History.* New York: Walker and Co., 1985.

Chronicle of Higher Education. 1255 23rd St. NW, Washington, D.C. 20037.

College Placement Council. *Spotlight, Journal of Career Planning and Employment, Salary Survey, CPC Annual,* and *CPC National Directory.*

Committee on History in the Classroom. *Teaching History.*

Committee on Lesbian and Gay History. *CGLH Newsletter.*

Conference of Historical Journals. *Editing History.*

Davis, Natalie Zemon; Penelope, Julia; Wolfe, Margery; Neverdon-Morton, Cynthia; and Gardiner, Linda, "Feminist Book Reviewing: A Symposium," *Feminist Studies,* vol. 14, no. 3, Fall 1988, 601-23.

Dissertation Abstracts. Ann Arbor, Mich.: University Microfilms International, Inc.

Dow Jones. *National Business Employment Weekly* .

Durgin, Rod W. *Guide to Federal Jobs.* Toledo, Ohio: Resource Directories, 1985.

Editorial Freelancers Association. *Newsletter.*

Federal Career Guide, R. B. Uleck Assoc., Gaithersburg, Md.

Federation of State Humanities Councils. *Humanities Discourse, Research Reports,* and *Federation of State Humanities Councils Directory.*

Groneman, Carol, and Robert N. Lear. *Corporate Ph.D.: Making the Grade in Business.* New York: Institute for Research in History/Facts on File, 1985.

Howe, Barbara J., and Emory L. Kemp., eds. *Public History: An Introduction.* Malabar, Fla.: Robert E. Krieger Publishing Co., 1986.

Hoy, Suellen, and Michael C. Robinson, eds. *Public Works History in the United States: A Guide to the Literature.* Nashville, Tenn.: American Association for State and Local History, 1982.

Lightman, Marjorie, and William Aeisel, eds. *Outside Academe: New Ways of Working in the Humanities.* New York: Institute for Research in History/Haworth Press, 1981.

LMP (*The Literary Marketplace*): *The Directory of American Book Publishing.* New York and London: R.R. Bowker & Co., published annually.

Malnig, Lawrence R., with Anita Malnig. *What Can I Do with a Major In . . . ? How to Choose and Use Your College Major.* Ridgefield, N.J.: Abbott Press, 1984.

McAdam, Terry W. *Careers in the Nonprofit Sector: Doing Well by Doing Good.* Washington, D.C.: The Taft Group, 1986.

National Association of Teachers' Agencies. *Bulletin* and *NATA.*
National Center for the Study of History, Inc. "Careers for Graduates in History" (1984), "Careers in Information Management for Graduates in the Liberal Arts: With Special Reference to Historians" (1986), and "Business & History" (1988).

National Coalition of Independent Scholars. *The Independent Scholar.*

National Council for the Social Studies. *Social Education* and *Social Studies Professional.*

National Council on Public History. *The Public Historian; Public History News; Guide to Continuing Education for Public Historians; Public History Education in America; Directory of Historical Consultants; Careers for Students of History* (with the American Historical Association); and special issues of *The Public Historian* on archives (vol. 8, 1986); business (vol. 3, Summer 1981); curriculum (vol. 9, Summer 1987); editing, publishing, and public history (vol. 4, Spring 1982); ethics (vol. 8, Winter 1986); National Park Service and historic preservation (vol. 9, Spring 1987); public history and local history (vol. 5, Fall 1983); public history in Europe (vol. 6, Fall 1984); and public history: state of the art (vol. 2, Winter 1980).

National Endowment for the Humanities. *Humanities.*

National Historical Publications and Records Commission. *Annotation.*

National Society for Internships and Experiential Education. *Experiential Education* and *The National Directory of Internships.*

National Trust for Historic Preservation. *Historic Preservation, Preservation News,* and an extensive list of publications from Preservation Press.

Neff, Glenda T. *Writer's Market,* Cincinnati, Ohio: Writer's Digest Books, 1990.

Oral History Association. *Oral History Review* and *Oral History Association Newsletter.*

Organization of American Historians. *Newsletter; Community College Network Newsletter; From Job Crisis to Job Opportunities: The OAH/FIPSE Project Careers Packet;* "Restoring Women to History: Teaching Packets for Integrating Women's History into Courses on Africa, Asia, Latin America, the Caribbean, and the Middle East." OAH Committee on Public History: *Teaching Public History to Undergraduates: A Guide for Departments of History; Educating Historians for Business: A Guide for Departments of History;* and *Historic Preservation: A Guide for Departments of History.*

Organization of History Teachers. *OHT Newsletter.*

Parsons, Paul. *Getting Published: The Acquisitions Process at University Presses.* University of Tennessee Press.

Peterson's Guides. *Peterson's Guide to Graduate and Professional Schools; Peterson's Guide to Independent Secondary Schools,* by Christopher Billy (1985); *Liberal Arts Jobs* (1985) and *Liberal Arts Power! How to Sell it on Your Résumé* (1986) by Jay Burton Nadler. Princeton, N.J.: Peterson's Guides.

Phifer, Paul. *College Majors and Careers: A Resource Guide for Effective Life Planning.* Garrett Park, Md.: Garrett Park Press, 1987.

Smithsonian Institution Office of Museum Programs and International Council of Museums' Committee for the Training of Personnel. Museum Studies International. Washington, D.C.: Smithsonian Institution, 1988.

Society for History Education, Inc. *The History Teacher.*

Society for History in the Federal Government. *The Federalist* and *Directory of Federal Historical Programs and Activities.*

Society for Scholarly Publishing. *Newsletter* and *Proceedings.*

Society of American Archivists. *American Archivist, SAA Newsletter,* and *Problems in Archives Kits (PAKS),* including "Finding an Archival Position: Résumés, Applications, Letters, and Interviews" (1981), "State/Local Government and Historical Societies" (1985), "College and University Archives" (1985), "Federal Archives and Miscellaneous Archives" (1985), and *Planning for the Archival Profession: A Report of the SAA Task Force on Goals and Priorities.* Chicago: Society of American Archivists (1986).

Vogel, Stephen E. *Directory of Employment Opportunities in the Federal Government.* New York: Arco Publishing, Inc., 1985.

Walkins, Mary Michelle, and James A. Ruffner, eds., *Research Centers Directory.* Detroit: Gale Research Co., 1983.

Western History Association. *The Western Historical Quarterly* and *Montana: The Magazine of Western History.*

Markus Wiener Publishers, 225 Lafayette St., S   11, New York, New York, 10012. For history teaching pack

A